THE VETERANS
SURVIVAL GUIDE

Related Titles from Brassey's

A Chain of Events: The Government Cover-up of the Black Hawk Incident and the Friendly-Fire Death of Lt. Laura Piper by Joan L. Piper

The Fate of America: An Inquiry into National Character by Michael Gellert

Legacy of Discord: Voices of the Vietnam War Era by Gil Dorland

Secrecy Wars: National Security, Privacy, and the Public's Right to Know by Philip H. Melanson

Silent Knights: Blowing the Whistle on Military Accidents and Their Cover-ups by Alan E. Diehl

When Dreams Came True: The GI Bill and the Making of Modern America by Michael J. Bennett

THE VETERAN'S SURVIVAL GUIDE

HOW TO FILE AND COLLECT ON VA CLAIMS

JOHN D. ROCHE

BRASSEY'S, INC.
Washington, D.C.

Published in the United States by Brassey's, Inc. All rights reserved. No part of
this book may be reproduced in any manner whatsoever without written permission
from the publisher, except in the case of brief quotations embodied in critical arti-
cles and reviews.

Typeset in Times Roman by World Composition Services, Inc., Sterling, VA

Library of Congress Cataloging-in-Publication Data

Roche, John D.
    The veteran's survival guide : how to file and collect on VA claims /
John D. Roche.—1st ed.
        p. cm.
Includes bibliographical references and index.
    ISBN 1-57488-415-8 (pbk. : alk. paper)
    1. Military pensions—Law and legislation—United States—Popular
works. 2. Veterans—Medical care—Law and legislation—United
States—Popular works. 3. Disabled veterans—Legal status, laws,
etc.—United States—Popular works. I. Title.
    KF7276.R63   2002
    331.25'291355'00973—dc21

                                                    2002002651

Printed in the United States of America on acid-free paper that meets the American
National Standards Institute Z39-48 Standard.

Brassey's, Inc.
22841 Quicksilver Drive
Dulles, Virginia 20166

First Edition

10   9   8   7   6   5   4   3   2   1

CONTENTS

PREFACE

Did you know that it takes four to five years for most claims processed by the Department of Veterans Affairs (VA) to be resolved? This book will give every veteran a chance to have his claim granted without being forced into the appeal process. Contrary to all the public relations hype on "how much we owe our veterans," "how we serve those who have served," or "putting customers first," the actual daily message being broadcast from Veterans Administration regional offices (VAROs) is too often "claim denied."

No matter how justified your claim to an entitlement is, you will lose if you expect the VA to jump in and help. If you expect the VA to tell you what you must do to have your claim approved, you will fail. Unless you know what to do, your claim most likely will be denied. The VA can do this simply by announcing you failed to submit a well-grounded claim.

The law allows you to appeal the decision, a process that usually takes three to five years of paper shuffling before the VA decides whether your claim is well grounded. Only after establishing that your claim was well grounded will the issue of the injury or disease be decided. If you are like most veterans, you will already have quit in frustration.

Do you believe the VAROs follow the law when dealing with your claim? Think again. If they did, why would you need a national network of service officers? Why is it necessary for every state and most counties, along with service organizations such as The American Legion, Veterans of Foreign Wars, and Disabled American Veterans, to pay someone to help you with the most basic aspects of applying for veterans benefits? Why is it necessary for the secretary of the VA to appoint sixty-five attorneys to the Board of Veterans' Appeals (BVA) to hear and adjudicate appeals generated by the denial of so many claims? The cost of operating the BVA was $37,679,000 in 1997 and $40,000,000 in 1999. Would there be a need for a United States Court of Appeals for Veterans Claims if the VAROs and the BVA did their jobs? This small administrative law court with its seven judges had an annual budget of $11 million in 1999.

The trend in the new Congress is to look at every government commitment as if it were part of a corporate balance sheet. If running an agency causes red ink, the solution is to change it, reduce it, or cut it. This new breed of politicians sees that approximately one-third of the nation's population—almost seventy million individuals, veterans, surviving spouses, dependent children, and parents—are potentially eligible for VA benefits or services. Recently released information (*VA Budget Facts 2001*) shows that 2.5 million veterans receive compensation benefits. Also receiving benefits were 1.1 million dependents. In fiscal year 2001, $15.8 billion in benefits was paid to veterans and dependents. The truly amazing fact is that this group represents only 10 percent of those possibly eligible for benefits.

Injuries and deaths resulting from treatment by the VA are classic examples of how bureaucrats manipulate entitlements. In 1934 the VA changed the language of the regulation (but not the law) to require veterans to prove negligence before benefits could be awarded. In 1988, a veteran named Gardner filed a claim based on negligent treatment by the VA. When his claim was denied, Mr. Gardner appealed the VA's decision all the way to the U.S. Supreme Court. The Court ruled that the VA had changed and administered the regulation illegally. The VA was reversed; however, it continues to fight every claim under Title 38 United States Code (U.S.C.) §1151 of the code with vigor.

True to the conservative pledge of allegiance to trim the cost, size, and services of the VA while still being able to be reelected or hold on to politically appointed top management positions, congressmen created many strategies to bring about major changes. Congress voted to allow the VA to charge many groups of veterans for their medical treatment and medication for non-service-related medical problems. The same act also allowed the VA to file claims against any health insurance policies a veteran owns.

In 1995, the VA contributed to the dismantling of benefits by restructuring the adjudication division as follows:

- Reduced grade levels for rating specialists from GS-12 and GS-13 to GS-9 to GS-12, which lowered the entry level of knowledge and experience required to evaluate claims
- Authorized single-signature rating decisions for almost every kind of claim action
- Removed medical doctors from membership on rating boards
- Scheduled veterans for general physical examinations only instead of specialized evaluations related to their medical problem
- Decided that non-VA staff general practitioners contracted on a fee-basis arrangement would conduct examinations for compensation benefits and authorized them to conduct specialized examinations in areas in which they have no expertise or training. Often these doctors were very old and long since retired from private practice or foreign-born doctors with limited English-language skills.

Chapter 4 discusses how VA medical policy affects veterans entitlement programs. With many of the old safeguards gone, single-member boards make entitlement decisions with limited understanding of the cause and effects of injuries and diseases. Unlike the previous system, there is no pooling of experience before a decision is rendered. With heavy caseloads and required daily performance standards, rating specialists have no time for research, detailed analysis, or application of court decisions for each claim.

Chief Judge Nebeker of the United States **Court of Appeals for Veterans Claims** publicly admonished the VA. The *American Legion Magazine* reported Judge Nebeker as saying, "The ROs [regional offices] were ignoring the law and precedent-setting court decisions and remands in their dealings with veterans claims." The article went on to quote the judge as saying, "VA policy is freely ignored by many initial adjudicators [ROs] whose attitude is 'I haven't been told by my boss to change. If you don't like it, appeal it.' "

Every veteran needs to understand how politicians and career high-level bureaucrats view veterans organizations as a source of influence. The first secretary of the VA, Edward J. Derwinski, appointed by President George Bush,[1] was quoted as saying, "Congress is dreadfully ignorant of the politics of veterans. They fear the veterans lobby but should not. The reality is they [veterans organizations] can't punch their way out of a paper bag." He added, "I wish I could have stayed another four years [because] I started to shake up the system."[2]

---

[1] Prior to the appointment of a secretary for the Department of Defense, the key individual was called the administrator.

[2] David Ballingrud and David Dahl, *St. Petersburg (Florida) Times,* 27 December 1997.

This secretary was also asked at one time by the United States Court of Appeals for Veterans Claims to show cause as to why he should not be cited for contempt of court for failure to comply with an order from the court.[3]

Your own claim has to survive a very unfriendly environment. Many elements will work against your claim. Nevertheless, you can beat the VA at its own game if you take the time to learn about the process and to document your medical problem. You must learn as much as you can about the type of claim you are filing and what the VA will require as proof.

---

[3] See *Moore v. Derwinski, 2 Vet. App. 67 (1992).*

ACKNOWLEDGMENTS

I owe a debt of gratitude to some very special people who volunteered their time and ideas to help me write this book. I am tremendously grateful to Robert Tralins for all his support and encouragement to write a book for veterans that would give them a leg up when dealing with the VA.

To Roland Wilson, my boss, who let me be a real advocate to those veterans who were my clients and not just a clerk filling out a form. Thank you for taking the heat when I stepped on the toes of bureaucrats and made them pay up.

I want to thank Rick Russell, my editor, for his insight and patience with a first-time writer who had more than his fair share of questions. I am truly lucky to have worked with you.

Finally, to my wife Patsy who always put the words I left out back into the manuscript. For your endless staying power, understanding, and wit in putting up with me for so many decades, love and bouquets forever.

INTRODUCTION

Over the past two decades, major political and economic priorities have altered the way the Department of Veterans Affairs (VA) does business. Within Congress, very few members are wartime veterans or ever served in the military services of the United States. From everything I have read, heard, and seen, the VA is looked upon by this new breed of lawmakers as one of the major contributors to the national debt. They liken it to a "social giveaway program" that dissipates public funds and receives nothing in return. Congress no longer embraces protection of benefits earned by members of the **armed forces**[1] as a sacred duty. No debt is owed for the hardships and sacrifices endured by those who serve. *The slate has been wiped clean.* Like apple pie, motherhood, and the American flag, however, no direct assault on veterans benefits is publicly possible.

These hidden attitudes of professional bureaucrats and politicians can be seen, however. In 1998, the VA's under secretary for Health asked Congress not to compensate or provide healthcare for veterans with disabilities resulting from smoking. The 1998 Republican Congress proved only too happy to oblige. In addition, Congress will not seek damages on behalf of veterans who are now disabled or dying because they were addicted to tobacco. Yet this same group of Congresspersons is going after a share of big tobacco money won by **states** to reimburse the cost of treating Medicaid patients for tobacco-related disorders.

---

[1] Bold terms are defined in Appendix C.

The VA's own Office of the General Counsel (OGC) had previously ruled in OGC Precedent Opinion 2-93 that **service connection** could be established for tobacco-related diseases. The number of **claims** filed citing addiction to tobacco that allegedly started while in the service may have prompted this request not to allocate funds.

Congress also made it mandatory to downsize the professional and administrative staff of the VA, and made protesting these changes a zero-discussion topic. To further entrench its destructive dismantling of the VA, Congress introduced an early retirement program that, in effect, encouraged the most highly skilled and knowledgeable employees to leave the service of the VA.

The rewards are great for those bureaucrats who do not resist the dismantling process. A case in point was the appointment of a former director of a VA **regional office** (VARO) to the position of executive director of a state Department of Veterans Affairs. He brought his former adjudication officer with him, who took the number two position in the state organization. These two men had been in charge of one of the worst-run VAROs in the country. Information released by the Department of Veterans Affairs' **Board of Veterans' Appeals** (BVA) identified this VARO as having a remand or reversed rate of almost 80 percent. How a former VA director and adjudication officer whose leadership earned them that type of recognition could become the voices for veterans whose claims are being denied is difficult to understand. Will such leadership help the cause of veterans? I doubt it. To be an advocate you have to be committed to challenge the system every step of the way, pursuing only the interest of the veteran who has asked for your help.

Let me illustrate a case that touches on almost all of these points. I once represented a female veteran who had major gynecological problems when she retired from the Marine Corps. She filed a claim for service-connected benefits two years after her **discharge** from the service. The VA scheduled her for a Compensation and Pension Examination (C&P Examination); however, because no gynecologist was employed at or by the VA medical center (VAMC), the VA authorized a nurse to conduct the examination. A bureaucracy that waives laws and licensing requirements and permits a nurse to assume the role of a doctor is flawed. Not surprisingly, the nurse's report provided no insight as to the seriousness of the veteran's condition. To make matters worse, the nurse failed to follow the protocol procedures set forth in VA Medical Manual IB 11 56, *Physician's Guide for Disability Evaluation Examinations*. In this case, the rating specialist should have returned the C&P Examination as being unsatisfactory, as required by regulations. Unfortunately, a reading of the rating **decision** revealed that the rating specialist did not understand or consider the significance of the medical evidence of record, so the claim was denied.

The client, at her expense, consulted a non-VA gynecologist. He received copies of her active duty medical records, 38 CFR §4.116(a), and the C&P Examination. He prepared an assessment of her condition at a **lay** level of medical understanding. Even with this new evidence, she still had to appeal the original decision. The VA eventually awarded her 100 percent compensation benefits for six months and a 50 percent disability rating for the remainder of her life.

By mid-1997, two major policy changes were announced: one by the under secretary for Health and the other by the

Benefits Administration. Both policies promised that the changes would benefit all veterans by bringing about major improvements within the VA.

In reality, the "New VA," as Under Secretary for Health Dr. Kenneth Kizer introduced his manifesto, has done very little for veterans. Until the Health Administration changes its policy and replaces part-time physicians and resident student doctors with full-time board-certified physicians currently licensed in the state where they are practicing, medical care will never rise above mediocrity. See chapter 6 for a more detailed discussion of exactly what I believe the "New VA" really means (i.e., another scheme to shave millions of dollars from the VA's annual budget).

The second big surprise in 1997 was the Muskogee VARO experiment that decentralized the adjudication function. In this test program, a management concept that eliminated almost all supervisory positions and replaced them with "empowered employees" replaced the concept of a supervisor held accountable for the progress of his sector. The new concept, which is referred to as "Influence vs. Authority: The Battle for Organizational Balance," is little more than an adult version of Dr. Spock's theory on child rearing and the idea that if you let a child do whatever it wants, it will achieve. Quoted in part from the VA's July 9, 1997, report at the National Conference on Federal Quality, Washington, D.C.:

Instead of automatic responses according to prescribed authority, this new generation of employees is being empowered to influence change by adding the value of their individual knowledge and creativity. . . . This approach eliminates authority-based positions in favor of self-management influence. . . . For the most part, mid-level management positions disappeared. . . . Outside recruitment went down to entry-level positions as merit promotions of lower-level employees went up.

This whole exercise is about cutting the cost of operating the VA and controlling the growth of entitlement programs.

The concept of self-management influence has a dark side, however. In early 1999, a veteran's claim supervisor who had been on the job for eleven years was charged with embezzling $600,000 by making false disability claims in the name of her fiancé. This supervisor took advantage of the opportunities for fraud, computer crimes, and flawed entitlement decisions that this management system created, all at the expense of veterans and the rest of the American people.

It's obvious from the results produced by single-signature rating actions and the excessive use of part-time, fee-basis, resident student doctors that veterans are getting the short end of the stick. This concept of influence versus authority will never elevate any VA employee to the experience and knowledge level of past rating boards that were composed of a physician, attorney, and occupational specialist. If the VA were truly serious about doing what is right for veterans, it would employ people with the skills needed to properly execute their job. It's pure fantasy to believe that you can take an individual with only the most basic education and experience and through the magic of "empowered employees" bring about a transformation that will allow him to resolve complex medical and legal questions to the satisfaction of all parties.

Life Cycle of Entitlements

The U.S. veterans benefits system traces its roots to the seventeenth century when the Pilgrims of Plymouth passed a law protecting citizens who joined the militia to defend the colony against the hostile Pequot Indians. The colony ensured that any soldier disabled in its defense would be supported by the colony.

When the colonies united and declared their independence from England, the Continental Congress of 1776 similarly addressed the needs of its soldiers. To encourage enlistments during the Revolutionary War, the Congress passed legislation authorizing pension benefits for soldiers. This was the first move by a fledgling republic to protect all citizens who took up arms to defend the republic.

The individual states and communities assumed responsibility for the medical and hospital care for veterans in the early days of the republic. In 1811, the federal government authorized the first domiciliary and medical facility for veterans. Throughout the 1800s the nation's veterans assistance program expanded to include benefits and pensions not only for veterans, but also for their widows and dependents.

Following the Civil War, many states established homes for their veterans. Veterans received medical and hospital treatment for all injuries and diseases, whether or not of service origin. Such homes cared for all homeless and disabled veterans of the Civil War, Indian Wars, Spanish-American War, and Mexican Border period, as well as those discharged from peacetime service.

When the United States entered World War I in 1917, Congress established a new system of veterans benefits. Programs included disability compensation, insurance for military members, and vocational rehabilitation for the disabled. The swelling ranks of veterans in the 1920s led to the administration of benefits by three federal agencies: the Veterans Bureau, the Bureau of Pensions of the Interior Department, and the National Home for Disabled Volunteer Soldiers. Yet veterans had to fend for themselves while dealing with three separate federal agencies, each with its own laws and regulations. Many veterans wandered from agency to agency because of confusion and contradiction within the agencies about who was in charge.

In 1930, Congress authorized the president to "consolidate and coordinate government activities affecting war veterans." The newly formed organization was known as the Veterans Administration. Congress reassigned the three agencies that formerly independently exercised control over veterans benefits to the Veterans Administration. Each became a bureau within the new organization.

The Department of Veterans Affairs was established as a cabinet-level position on March 15, 1989. President George Bush hailed the creation of the new department, saying, "There is only one place for the veterans of America, in the Cabinet Room, at the table with the President of the United States of America." The first secretary of the VA was a former Republican congressman named Derwinski. Contrary to President Bush's statement regarding the recognition of the VA, however, nothing of momentous proportion has yet to escape from the president's cabinet room to benefit veterans at large.

Despite the rhetoric of "We can't do enough for you" that has bombarded veterans since the early 1980s, benefits are constantly being downsized. Since Ronald Reagan's presidency, the majority parties in Congress have measured veterans' benefits only by bottom-line costs. Gone are the pledges of a nation grateful for the sacrifices of those who have served. When politicians look at the fact that nearly 27 million people served in the military—and in theory each has a potential claim for benefits—they see an immediate threat to their special-interest projects.

It would appear un-American for any politician to blatantly announce cuts in benefits for veterans—one might as well attack motherhood, apple pie, or the flag—so they have downsized the VA, reduced its operating budget, and caused early retirement for senior claims and rating **board members**. Now claims drag on endlessly before a decision is reached, and the low level of technical skill by the new generation of rating boards and claim examiners results in a higher rate of denial of benefits. There has also been an effort to make VA compensation benefits taxable, which if voted into law, would reduce the spendable income of the disabled. Some veterans must pay for their medication from the VA if the prescription is not directly linked to a service-connected condition. Veterans treated for anything other than a service-connected illness or disease, and whose income is greater than the poverty level, must pay for their care. If they have a private insurance company, their care could be charged against their policy. Furthermore, because the VA cannot compete for highly skilled physicians, it hires many foreign doctors who will work at a low salary. The VA accepts language limitations in an effort to maintain hospital staffing requirements. The VA has reduced the configuration and size of rating boards: doctors are no longer members of the board, and one person decides just about every type of claim considered by the former three-member board. These individuals are not medically or legally trained. Very few, if any, have the ability to evaluate complex medical issues requiring specialized training and experience.

The only event in 1989 that was truly helpful for veterans was the establishment of the United States Court of Appeals for Veterans Claims. The VA was no longer free to interpret its laws and regulations as it saw fit. No longer could the VA act as its own judge and jury regarding veterans' claims and benefits. The new federal court's only purpose was to ensure that the laws and regulations pertaining to veterans benefits were properly and fairly administered. After seven long years, in 1989 the court finally began reshaping the review process by the BVA. Yet the BVA is reversing and remanding **appeals** from VAROs nationwide at an astounding rate of 70 percent. Such a high rate means that the reforms did not work and that the VAROs are still not doing a good job.

Only a small percentage of veterans ever exercise their right of appeal. If every veteran who was turned down appealed the denial of benefits, that percentage would shoot up. VAROs continue to ignore the decisions of the court; they fail to follow the regulations and laws; and they are not deciding claims based on precedent-setting case law mandated by the court.

Before filing any type of claim action with the VA, you need to know basic fundamental concepts. Jesse Brown, former secretary of the VA, claims that the VA is user friendly. He was quoted in the *American Legion Magazine* in 1995 as saying he does "not believe that the Veterans Benefits Administration was systematically ignoring the law or the court." He did not say, "I *know* they are not ignoring the law or the courts." For this reason, you must take the time to understand how the VA operates, what its responsibilities are, and what proof you need for your claim. So, if you have not read the introduction to this book, do so now. There are no shortcuts when it comes to filing a claim for your VA benefits.

Nine Types of Claim Actions

A veteran can **file** many types of claim actions with the VA. This book focuses on the four most important service-connected claim actions that a veteran can file. It is absolutely necessary to know exactly what is entailed for the benefit you are claiming. You must know what the law requires for each category of claim before it is submitted, as each category of claim action has special development techniques. For example, a common mistake is to ask to "reopen" a claim when you really want to "amend" the claim. To receive the benefits that are owed you, you must know what you want to claim and what the VA's responsibility is in responding to your request.

The nine categories of claims are

- informal claim
- compensation claim
- reopened claim
- claim for 100 percent total disability due to individual unemployability
- claim for an increased rating due to a change in the severity of your service-connected condition
- adjunct or secondary disabilities to original service-connected disability
- claim for service connection for conditions resulting from medical treatment at VA hospital or clinics
- survivor's dependency and indemnity compensation claim
- **non-service-connected** pension claims

Ground Rules to Win By

Rules that shape a winning claim action are briefly discussed below. A successful claimant must have a basic understanding of what is involved in the development of a claim. Nearly all the topics discussed below are examined in detail in later chapters.

WELL-GROUNDED CLAIM A MUST

The VA will dismiss any claim action it perceives as not being well grounded. You have the duty to submit evidence sufficient to justify a belief by a fair and impartial individual that the claim is plausible or capable of substantiation. This means that you cannot just go into the VA with a claim application stating, "I hurt my back in the service. The intervertebral disc syndrome that now has me totally disabled twenty years after leaving the service is the result of an active duty injury." Simply claiming that your medical condition is the result of an active duty injury will not qualify your claim as being well grounded.

Until you have met this first requirement, the law does not require the VA to assist you in developing your claim.[1] Therefore, you must know how to prove your claim. Failure to do so will result in a denial of your claim. If you stick it out, you'll be in for a three- to five-year battle establishing only one issue—that your claim was well grounded. Assuming you are successful in eventually proving your claim was well grounded, the VA will then go back to square one and look at all available evidence and decide if service connection for

---

[1] See chapters 9 and 10 for case law decisions that clarify the issue of a well-grounded claim and the VA's duty to assist.

your alleged injury is warranted. Should your claim be denied or underrated, you will have to start the appeal process all over again, which means another three- to five-year wait. As you can see, a decade could pass before a decision is made on a hastily filed claim action. The question you must ask yourself is, "Will I be alive once the claim runs its course?" Do it right the first time: make certain your claim is well grounded and that there is evidence to support your contention that you were indeed injured or became sick in the service. See chapter 9 for a detailed discussion concerning a well-grounded claim.

NO RECORDS, NO CLAIM

If you do not have copies of your active duty outpatient or inpatient medical records, you must obtain them. Outpatient medical records and military hospital records are maintained separately at the National Personnel Records Center (NPRC) in St. Louis, Missouri. Outpatient records are kept with your administrative and personnel records, and inpatient records are stored in the hospital records section. When requesting a search for hospital records, you'll be asked to provide your full name, military serial number, the military unit you were assigned to at the time of hospitalization, the name and location of the hospital, the dates you were hospitalized, and the reason for the hospitalization.

In the mid-1950s, millions of World War II and Korean War Army hospital records were turned over to the VA as part of a special study. When the project was finished, the VA did not return the records to the NPRC, but placed them in storage where they were forgotten. It was not until the late 1980s that this fact was made public. If you were advised that there were no hospital records at the NPRC, and you were hospitalized overseas for a combat wound, injury, or disease, contact the VA and request a copy of your records.

Under the 1996 memorandum of understanding between the Department of Defense and the Department of Veterans Affairs, medical records of all military members retiring or separating after May 1, 1994, are transferred directly to the VA rather than to the NPRC. The agreement calls for each military branch to forward medical records to the VA Medical Record Center, St. Louis, Missouri, for those members not initiating a claim. If the member initiates a claim during outprocessing, his medical records will be transferred directly to the VARO closest to his future address.

HOW THE VA RATES AN INJURY OR DISEASE

When all the medical facts evidencing your claim have been gathered, the evidence is cross-referenced against Title 38 Code of Federal Regulations (CFR) Part 4, Schedule for Rating Disabilities. This section of the CFR lists the medical problems that the VA rates as service connected.

Because this section of the 38 CFR has not been updated since 1945, there are no rating descriptions for many new disabling diseases. An "analogous rating" is made, which simply means that an injury or disease that is closely related is used. This decisionmaking process by a rating board member is highly subjective. Ratings given under this procedure should be carefully scrutinized. You can recognize these ratings by the last two numbers in the four-digit rating code: 99.

Before you submit a claim for a particular medical problem, obtain a copy of 38 CFR Part 4 and compare your medical condition to the rating schedule for that condition. The schedule will tell you what the medical facts must show before the VA will grant service connection.

TESTIMONIAL EVIDENCE A MUST

To make sure you have **probative evidence** of an injury or disease, you must know how to prepare sworn written testimony supporting the claim. The VA is quick to disregard buddy letters as evidence. However, a properly executed deposition giving a detailed explanation of pertinent facts from you, members of your family, fellow employees, employer, or former military comrades is vital **relevant** evidence. The VA can disregard your sworn statements only if it has hard factual evidence to the contrary. Although it may not want to, the VA must give this type of evidence considerable weight. You must learn how to construct these statements so they relate facts, not opinions or conjecture. The deposition must demonstrate how your medical condition affects your daily routine in the workplace.

THE ADJUDICATION PROCESS: THE WEAK LINK

The working rules are translated from laws passed by Congress—they are not arbitrary rules that claim examiners and rating board members create, ignore, or change at will. However, VAROs, contrary to former Secretary Jesse Brown's belief, violate the law all the time. If he examined the number of cases returned to the regional offices by the BVA, he certainly could not publicly state that he believed that the "Veterans Benefit Administration was not systematically ignoring the law or the court."[2]

---

[2] "Judge Chastises VA Regional Offices," *American Legion Magazine,* Jan–Feb 1995.

Let me illustrate an incident that occurred at a training session for state and county service officers. During the adjudication officer's question-and-answer session, I asked him why veterans were being scheduled for C&P Examinations when the doctor did not have the **claim file**. He explained that the VA was not required to provide the claim file unless it was for a psychiatric examination. I pushed him a little harder, reminding him that 38 CFR requires that the file be available to the doctor for review before the examination. Then I added that the *Physician's Guide for Disability Evaluation Examinations* tells the doctor exactly what should be reviewed in the claim file and why. He restated his answer. I then reminded him that the courts ruled that the claim file must be available to the examining physician to ensure a thorough and contemporaneous examination. He turned away and took no more comments from me.

Very few veterans are aware that their claim file must be reviewed and made part of the examination by the doctor. It is the duty of the rating specialist requesting the examination to ensure that the hospital or clinic has the file before the examination occurs. (See chapter 5 for a complete discussion of C&P Examinations.)

To ensure a just and fair decision on your claim, you must understand what the law requires of rating board members during the adjudication process. Unless you are knowledgeable about what takes place during this process, it's very likely that your claim will be denied or, if granted, the award may be considerably less than what your disability justifies.

IN THE LINE OF DUTY, OR BENEFITS DENIED

Determining whether your injury or disease was the result of **willful misconduct** is one of the first actions a rating specialist will take. For instance, did your organization conduct a line-of-duty investigation surrounding the circumstances of your injury or illness? If the investigating officer finds that your medical problem or injury was caused while **in the line of duty,** those findings are binding on the VA. In accordance with 38 CFR §3.1(n), the VA must accept the service department decision as binding.

The exception to the rule occurs when the VA can prove the ruling was patently inconsistent with the facts and the laws administered by the VA. Keep in mind that all active duty members are on duty twenty-four hours a day, seven days a week, fifty-two weeks a year. Thus everything they did was in the line of duty, unless it involved deliberate or intentional wrongdoing with wanton and reckless disregard of its probable consequences.

When a claim is made and there was no line-of-duty investigation concerning the incident, a problem is likely to arise. When the circumstances surrounding your injury or disease are left to the interpretation of a rating specialist, the decision could be based on facts not in evidence, thereby resulting in a denial of benefits.

Safeguards built into the regulation are designed to protect you from indiscriminate denial of benefits because of mere technical violation of civil ordinances. Such circumstances per se do not constitute willful misconduct. The regulation also points out that willful misconduct will not be determinative unless it is the **proximate cause** of injury, disease, or death.

If your claim is denied on the basis of willful misconduct, the VA must give you a detailed account of how it arrived at this conclusion. If the explanation does not discuss the evidence used in determining willful misconduct and how the VA arrived at this decision, the VA is in violation of its own regulations. At this point you must appeal the denial of benefits.

PRESUMPTION OF SOUNDNESS: A KEY ISSUE

The governing regulations dealing with the issue of presumption of soundness are 38 CFR §3.304(b) and 38 CFR §3.305(b). Both regulations state that a veteran will be considered to have been in sound condition when examined, accepted, and enrolled for service except as to the defects, infirmities, and disorders noted on the entrance examination. *When* the claimant entered the service is the difference between the two regulations. Regulation 38 CFR §3.304(b) addresses those claims filed on and after January 1, 1947, whereas 38 CFR §3.305(b) covers claims filed before January 1, 1947. There is one other important difference between the two regulations. Individuals on active duty before January 1, 1947, had to serve on active duty at least six months before the presumption-of-soundness policy applied to their claim. For those who served after that date, the presumption applied immediately.

The law provides that any defects, infirmities, or disorders noted during the entry examination will not be considered a service-related condition unless they suffered aggravation (worsened). Both regulations stipulate that there must be clear and unmistakable (obvious or manifest) evidence that demonstrates that the injury or disease existed before entry into the service. A key point to remember is that only those medical conditions recorded on the entrance examination can be considered as preexisting. An isolated reference in the medical file alleging that a condition existed before service cannot be the sole basis for denial of benefits.

The United States Court of Appeals for Veterans Claims has

addressed the issues of denial of benefits based on preexisting medical conditions and presumption of soundness on several occasions. The case of *Parker v. Derwinski, 1 Vet. App. 522 (1992)* illustrates how the VA deviates from regulations by applying its own interpretation to issues.

Mr. Parker sought to reopen his claim for disability benefits based on alleged vision deficiency caused by a hole in his left eye. The VA position in justifying the denial of service connection was based on the absence of any indication of trauma during active duty, and an unsubstantiated statement by an army doctor referring to an alleged injury when Parker was 19 years old. The VA concluded that this evidence was sufficient to **rebut** the presumption-of-soundness rule.

To prevail, the VA has to prove that a preexisting injury or disease had been demonstrated by unmistakable evidence. The VA submitted two pieces of evidence to support its position: a statement from an Army doctor alleging Mr. Parker injured his eye playing football at age 19, and the fact that service medical records were silent as to an injury to the left eye. The court pointed out that Mr. Parker's sworn statement and the statements of several doctors in evidence were ignored by the VA. The court vacated the VA decision and **remanded** it to the regional office for readjudication.

This particular veteran's claim was handicapped by the fact that he waited ten years before filing his original claim for service connection. His initial claim was denied, and he filed no appeal. In 1987, after waiting another ten years, he tried to reopen his claim based on new and material evidence, but his request was promptly denied. Again he did not appeal the denial. Each time he tried to reopen his claim he included one new letter from a friend or doctor. In 1989, after receiving another denial to reopen his claim, he filed a timely appeal. It wasn't until 1991 that his appeal made its way to the Court of Appeals for Veterans Claims.

This case is an excellent example of how a claim can be dragged out for decades. When you file your claim, do not assume the VA will gather the evidence to support your contentions. This is *your* job. If you do take the easy way out and file only an application with the hope the VA will gather the evidence, you will lose.

Any time your claim is denied, you should file a **Notice of Disagreement** to appeal the decision. The rating board members and claim specialist in every VARO across this country make thousands of errors each year. Do not accept a denial— do something about it. File a Notice of Disagreement to appeal the decision. But don't stop there.

CHRONIC DISEASES

A chronic disease must manifest itself to a degree of 10 percent or more within one year of the date of separation from the service. However, there are several exceptions to this rule. If leprosy or tuberculosis develops to a 10 percent level of disability within three years, or multiple sclerosis within seven years, then service connection under this rule will be granted.

The key word is "manifest" and is not the same as being diagnosed. The condition qualifies as manifest if it can be shown that during the year following separation the symptoms for the condition equate to the 10 percent rating for the disease as stated in 38 CFR Part 4, Schedule for Rating Disabilities. No condition other than the forty diseases named in 38 CFR §3.309(a) (and listed below) will be considered chronic under the **presumptive** rule. The chronic diseases are

anemia, primary
arteriosclerosis
arthritis
atrophy, progressive muscular
brain hemorrhage
brain thrombosis
bronchiectasis
calculi of the kidney, bladder, or gallbladder
cardiovascular-renal disease, including hypertension
cirrhosis of the liver
coccidioidomycosis
diabetes mellitus
encephalitis lethargica **residuals**
endocarditis (all forms of valvular heart disease)
endocrinopathies
epilepsies
Hansen's disease
Hodgkin's disease
leukemia
lupus erythematosus, systemic
myasthenia gravis
myelitis
myocarditis
nephritis
other organic diseases of the nervous system
osteitis deformans (Paget's disease)
osteomalacia
palsy, bulbar
paralysis agitans
psychoses
purpura, idiopathic, hemorrhagic
Raynaud's disease

sarcoidosis
scleroderma
sclerosis, amyotrophic lateral
sclerosis, multiple
syringomyelia
thromboangiitis obliterans (Buerger's disease)
tuberculosis, active
tumor, malignant, or of the brain, spinal cord, or
   peripheral nerves
ulcers, peptic, gastric, or duodenal

TROPICAL DISEASES

The tropics have always presented a serious medical hazard for
military members. Realizing this, Congress presumes service
connection for sixteen diseases and resultant disorders. It also
recognizes that treatment or preventative measures for many
of these diseases could cause adjunct disabilities.

However, Congress also wrote into the law a **rebuttal rule**
that the VA must satisfy before presumptive service connection
can be granted. The claim can be denied if the VA can show
that the individual didn't serve in a locality with a high inci-
dence rate of the disease or a continuous occurrence in the
local population. It can also be denied if the claimant separated
from the service beyond the known incubation periods for the
tropical disease.

One of the sixteen diseases in this presumptive group is
amebiasis, a disease that is generally characterized by dysentery
with diarrhea, weakness, and prostration. The disease may stay
in remission for several years after exposure. The first symptom
is often diagnosed as a stomach virus and treated accordingly.

When the patient doesn't respond to the standard treatment normally given for a stomach virus, the doctor usually orders a more serious study. At this point, the findings usually show the individual as being disabled by amebae. The patient then learns from his doctor that his chronic condition is not common where he lives, and he is also advised that the disease is not known to be a common health problem at his last duty station. He is told that it is common in the tropics—such as in Southeast Asia—and is acquired by ingesting food or drink containing encysted forms.

Then the patient recalls that just before his discharge, he was on temporary duty for one week in Saigon, South Vietnam. He and his friends toured the local sights and ate and drank in local restaurants. He files a claim that is promptly denied by the VA on the basis of not being well grounded. The claimant's medical records do not establish treatment for the condition on active duty. His service records show he was never stationed in any tropical regions where the disease was prevalent. His records also establish he was discharged over two years ago.

This claim is winnable, but the claimant must properly develop it before filing a formal application. In this situation, he should file an informal claim to protect the date and serve **notice** that a service-connected disability claim will be forthcoming. (The various types of claim actions are discussed in chapter 3.)

Three sections within 38 CFR Part 3 govern the awarding of service connection for one of the sixteen tropical diseases presumed to be service connected if they manifest to a degree of 10 percent within a year of separating from the service. The first requirement outlined in 38 CFR §3.309(b) identifies the sixteen diseases. Next, 38 CFR §3.307(a)(1)(4) requires a veteran to have served at least ninety days after December 31,

1946, and that the disease manifested to a degree of 10 percent or more within one year from date of separation. The third condition outlined in 38 CFR §3.308(b) requires a veteran who separated before January 1, 1947, to serve at least six months on active duty before becoming eligible for presumptive service connection. The veteran must also show that the disease existed to a degree of 10 percent within one year of separating from the service.

An exception applies to all three sections of the law: if the incubation period commenced during the service, establishing presumptive service connection for any one of the diseases shown below is not limited to the disease manifesting to a degree of 10 percent or more within one year from separation. If you have contracted one of these diseases you must ask your physician about the incubation period, the disease cycle between an active state and remission once you've been exposed, the existence of permanent cures, and the prevalence of the disease where you lived after leaving the service or where you were stationed.

38 CFR §3.309(b) identifies the following presumptive diseases as tropical:

amebiasis
blackwater fever
cholera
dracontiasis
dysentery
filariasis
leishmaniasis including kala-azar
loiasis
malaria
onchocerciasis

Oroya fever
pinta
plague
schistosomiasis
yaws
yellow fever

Service connection will also be established for secondary medical problems originating from the original disease or for medical problems originating from the required therapy.

CHRONICITY

The VA recognizes forty diseases as chronic disorders for which service connection may be granted. To determine if your medical problem is considered by the VA as a chronic disorder, consult 38 CFR §3.309(a) and Part 4.

If you were diagnosed and treated for a chronic condition on active duty or within the one-year presumptive period after leaving the service, you should have filed a claim during that time. In order to establish service connection for a chronic disease, there must be sufficient evidence to identify the disease along with ample observation to establish **chronicity**. The record has to establish that the diagnosis was not a mere isolated finding or that the diagnosis includes the word "chronic." If you meet this test, later occurrences of this condition—no matter how remote—will be considered service connected. Let's say you had a condition that was in remission when you left the service and remained that way for another ten years. You could establish service connection on the basis of chronicity without having to prove continuity of symptomatology.

However, there is an exception to the rule: if the VA can show that the current symptoms and diagnosis are attributable to intercurrent causes (two or more illnesses occurring at the same time), then service connection will be denied. Under 38 CFR §3.303(b), "This rule does not mean that any manifestation of joint pain, any abnormality of heart action or heart sounds, any urinary findings of casts, or any cough, in service will permit service connection of arthritis, disease of the heart, nephritis, or pulmonary disease, first shown as a clear-cut clinical entity, at some later date."

CONTINUITY OF SYMPTOMATOLOGY

A claim for service connection becomes extremely difficult to establish under the rule of continuity of symptomatology when you have been separated from the service for many years. VA regulations state that continuity of symptomatology is required only when the condition noted during service—or during the one-year presumptive period following separation—is not, in fact, shown to be chronic, or when the diagnosis of chronicity may be legitimately questioned.

To prove continuity of symptomatology, a record of continuous medical treatment must be introduced into evidence showing that you were under continuous treatment for the disability you are claiming. The example I like to use when helping clients visualize the immense undertaking at hand is the completion of a bridge spanning a very wide river. On one side of the river is a completed on-ramp that represents your active duty medical records. On the other side of the river is the completed off-ramp that represents the current treatment record of your injury. Your job is to figure how to span the river and connect the ramps. Without the proper material and engineering plans, you cannot complete the bridge. Without sufficient medical evidence to support continuity of symptomatology, your claim will be denied.

Medical evidence necessary to prove your claim may no longer be accessible or obtainable. The most common reasons for this situation arc

- the inability to retrieve old medical records
- not being able to remember the doctor's name
- forgetting where and when treatment for the problem occurred
- death of the doctor who treated the veteran
- destruction of the medical treatment records because the veteran was no longer a patient or because the doctor sold his practice or retired

As a claimant you must understand that when the fact of chronicity in service is not adequately supported, you must prove continuity after separation before a claim can be successfully prosecuted. (See chapter 7 for ways to develop a claim under the continuity rule.)

COMBAT RELATED INJURIES AND DISEASES

Official records or documents are not required to support your claim if you are a combat veteran and you file a claim for injuries or disease incurred or aggravated while engaged in wartime operations against **hostile forces**. The VA is required to accept satisfactory lay or other evidence as the basis for the claim, as long as the evidence is consistent with the circumstances, conditions, or hardships of such service.

This rule does not mean that you had to have direct physical contact with enemy forces before a claim is justified. Being assigned to a combat unit conducting tactical operations during a declared wartime, or during undeclared wartime engagements such as campaigns or expeditions supporting the United States or the United Nations for diplomatic purposes, qualifies. Operations such as those in Grenada, the Persian Gulf, or Panama, or temporary assignment to U.N. Forces, as in Bosnia, qualify under this rule.

Your sworn statement of the events surrounding the injury or illness is in most cases sufficient for establishing a well-grounded claim. Sworn statements from members of your unit are also acceptable evidence in establishing the basis of a well-grounded claim when there are no medical records to support your claim. This rule is extremely important for veterans who served in a combat zone. Proof of being awarded the Purple Heart or Combat Infantryman Badge can establish your presence in a combat zone. Obtaining a copy of the official unit history during the period when you were wounded or became ill is considered proof your claim is combat related. Proof of being awarded various medals associated with combat operations such as the Bronze Star, Silver Star, Distinguished Flying Cross, and the Air Medal is excellent evidence establishing your presence in a combat zone.

In a special case, *Collette v. Brown, 95-7043 (1996),* the United States Court of Appeals for the Federal Circuit reversed the Court of Veterans Appeals on the issue of what veterans must prove if they allege combat injuries are the basis of the claim. The Court of Appeals for the Federal Circuit held that the VA must accept the veteran's **lay evidence** (a statement that the injury or disease occurred in combat), unless it has proof to the contrary. The only evidence veterans need is proof that they were engaged in combat with the enemy. The decision is absolutely binding on all VAROs.

Chapter 1 Highlights

For more than three hundred years, the law of the land has decreed that those who were wounded, injured, or diseased in the defense of this country would be provided with the care and financial assistance necessary to go on with their lives. As the ranks of those who served this country by taking up arms either to defend it from a hostile enemy or to enforce our national political agenda swell, the number of individuals disabled by this service also has sharply increased. In the 20th century, this country sent its young people into harm's way more than ten times.

Our military members have been used in testing biochemical agents and nuclear radiation and in other experiments without their knowledge or permission. Since World War I our country has deserted thousands of American troops who were missing in action by declaring them Killed in Action/Body Not Recovered. There has been no real aggressive action by this country to follow leads and account for these individuals. That isn't to say they haven't spent millions of dollars in the quest for "answers." Our government and politicians deserve high marks in producing catchy slogans and speeches expressing their compassion for the plight of these people.

The bottom line is this: The problem is not the expense of sending the American military into combat, it's the cost of supporting those who survived the wars, police actions, and the dangers of daily military duty. The politicians want to cut the costs of this country's obligation to its veterans, but they do so covertly by reorganizing the internal structure of the VA in the name of streamlining management. They're changing the structure of rating boards by eliminating physicians and attorneys from the boards and allowing an individual without a medical or legal background to decide the merits of complex claims. They're reducing the hospital medical staff and hiring foreign doctors and retired physicians. The law does not require a doctor to be licensed or recognized by the state in which the

VA facility is located in order to practice medicine. To get a job as a doctor with the VA, all that is required is a medical degree from any school in the world. Additional cost-saving measures include allowing part-time resident doctors from local hospitals and physician's assistants to treat veterans and evaluate their medical claims.

Remember, to file a well-grounded claim, know what makes a well-grounded claim, where to look for records, and how to execute sworn statements. Also keep in mind the following points:

- Anything that happens to you on active duty is service related unless you had a wanton disregard for safety or were involved in a felonious criminal act.
- If your entrance physical examination is silent as to a medical condition existing before joining the service, then it is presumed that you were in perfect health when sworn in.
- Make certain that when you are examined for compensation benefits the VA doctor has your claim folder and has reviewed it before the exam.
- Chronicity or continuity of symptoms must exist if the claim is filed more than one year after leaving the service.
- The VA must accept a combat veteran's explanation as to the circumstances of his injury or disease unless it has solid evidence that rebuts the veteran's account of the facts.

Knowing Where to Look for "Denied" Signs

A veteran can establish service connection for an injury or disease by claiming that a preexisting condition was aggravated, that an injury or disease was a direct result of service, or that an existing service-connected condition has become more severe. The first step is to ask, "Is this disability the result of a condition that happened *before* or *after* entering the service?"

If the disability you are claiming was preexisting—and is so noted on your entry physical examination—the question you need to focus on is "Was the condition asymptomatic when I entered?" If you were symptom free when you entered, you would base your claim on aggravation of a preexisting condition. However, if you were given a medical waiver for entry into the service for this preexisting condition, you will have to prove that during your period of service, the condition increased in severity beyond the natural course of the disease. Because your compensation benefits are going to be based on this difference, this consideration is very important.

When you are claiming service connection for an injury or disease that occurred while on duty, the action is straightforward and fairly uncomplicated. To protect your rights and receive the greatest advantage, file your claim within one year after leaving the service. By doing so, the entitlement date for benefits will be the day following your date of separation; you won't have much difficulty proving the disability occurred in the service; and your claim will be considered well grounded, thereby triggering the VA's duty to assist.

Some basic diseases may surface anywhere from one to forty years after leaving the service. These are called "presumptive diseases," and as long as they manifest to a degree of 10 percent or more within this time frame, they will be rated as service connected. If you have a chronic tropical disease or a condition associated with radiation exposure, Agent Orange, the Persian Gulf War, or being a prisoner of war (POW), you may be entitled to service-connected benefits.

The next special consideration you must focus on is what you must do if the injury or disease was related to events that occurred while you were on active duty. The law says the VA must consider each disabling condition on the basis of the place, types, and circumstances of your service as shown by service records. It must consider the official history of each organization you served in, your medical records, and all other pertinent medical and lay evidence. Most important, service connection will be based on a review of all the evidence of record. Your evidence will be given a broad and liberal interpretation consistent with the facts of the claim as dictated by Congress.

This duty is the VA's as clearly defined in the law and federal regulations. Unfortunately, the VA does not always fulfill its duty. In all the claim files I have reviewed, I never saw documents requested from the Defense Department that related to the military history of the claimant's unit. There was never any evidence in the files that clearly showed what type of impact a military assignment had on the alleged condition.

Along these same lines, if you tell the VA that you were

treated at VA hospitals in other states, the regional office is required to get these records. But when you look in the file, you won't find evidence of this request for information. If you know where you were treated within the VA medical system, request copies of the records yourself. You cannot be refused. Just because the law says the VA is supposed to take this action on your behalf, do not assume that it will.

Statistics released in 1995 by the BVA show that the remand and reversal rate of regional office decisions ranges between 75 and 79 percent. In other words, regional offices' decisions are only 20 percent reliable. These figures represent only those claims that were denied and appealed by the claimants. They do not consider the millions of individuals who were denied benefits and gave up without filing an appeal.

I have a letter from a director of one regional office to my congressional representative that reveals the VA has no way of identifying the number of cases that are approved or disapproved. This director could cite the number of claims processed during a given period, but he could not tell how many claims were pending. With computerized recordkeeping at such an advanced level, it's strange that a regional office does not have the capability of recording the number of claims it approves or denies. On the other hand, the BVA will tell you how many appeals they have from each regional office, the number of VARO decisions they uphold, the number they reverse, and the number they remand to the VAROs to be reworked for compliance with the regulations and laws.

Road Block One: Preexisting Conditions

The VA maintains that there are medical principles so universally recognized that no additional proof is necessary to deny the claim. For example, a notation recorded on Standard Form (SF) 93, Report of Medical History, states that if a preservice medical examination reveals frequent incapacitation by asthma attacks as a child, denial of benefits is almost a certainty. In the initial review of a claim, the VA probably will not consider the fact that the preservice medical examination shows no evidence of residuals or physical limitation resulting from this childhood asthmatic condition. Under these circumstances, you must base your claim on the aggravation of a preexisting condition.

However, 38 CFR §3.303(c) also prompts the VA to deny any claim that indicates the existence of a chronic disease from date of entry into service if the disease could not have originated during the first few months of service. Diseases of an infectious nature are considered with regard to the circumstances of the infection. The VA holds that the condition preexisted the service if the symptoms appear in less than the incubation period after reporting for active duty. For example, a claim for chronic inflammation of the middle ear (otitis media) would be denied if the medical records confirmed that the veteran was hospitalized for scarlet fever on the second day of basic training. Scarlet fever has an incubation period of three to four days. A rating board member would conclude that the chronic middle ear infection was the residual effect of scarlet fever. For the veteran to prevail in a case like this he would have to prove that his chronic otitis media resulted from a condition other than scarlet fever, such as an allergy, fungus, or proteus (bacteria).

The regulations also stipulate that congenital or developmental defects—such as refractive eyesight error, personality disorders, and mental deficiency—are *not* diseases or injuries within the meaning of the law. Many young people are discharged from the service in the very early stages of training as unadaptable because of a preexisting "personality disorder." The military will immediately remove anyone from its training program who doesn't conform to its expectations of a soldier, sailor, Marine, or airman. In many cases the discharge is justified based on a diagnosis of a personality disorder. Yet the training can be very traumatic and can itself trigger a preexisting psychotic or psychoneurotic disorder that mirrors many of the same symptoms of a personality disorder. An individual disabled by a personality disorder would not be entitled to benefits by law. But, if a preexisting neurotic or psychotic disorder existed, the veteran might be entitled to benefits based on aggravation of a preexisting condition.

Road Block Two: Service-Related Conditions

Service connection will be granted for any disease diagnosed after separation when all the evidence, including that which is pertinent to the service, establishes that the disease or injury was incurred in the service. It was also the intent of Congress to create a **presumptive period** for certain diseases: if manifested to a **compensable** degree within the presumptive period, direct service connection will be granted. (The presumptive rule is discussed in chapter 1.) This presumptive provision of the statute is intended to relax the rating guidelines when the evidence would not otherwise warrant service connection. If the disease is considered at least 10 percent disabling within the presumptive period, those diseases listed in 38 CFR §3.309, 38 CFR §3.310, and 38 CFR §3.311 will be deemed incurred in the service even though there is no evidence of such disease during active duty.

When a postservice claim is filed that does not qualify under the presumptive rule, the test of service connection will be based on the rule of "continuity of symptomatology." (The concept of continuity of symptomatology is discussed in chapter 1.)

Road Block Three: Medical Problems Caused by the VA

The policy for injuries or disease resulting from hospital or medical care by the VA is set forth in 38 U.S.C. §1151 and three codified regulations: 38 CFR §3.154, 38 CFR §3.400(i), and 38 CFR §3.800(a). The policy describing an 1151 claim states that the VA will accept an informal or formal claim showing intent to claim a disability or death as a basis of medical treatment. The policy includes claims from veterans receiving treatment for non-service-related health problems and those veterans who are enrolled in vocational rehabilitation. The United States Court of Appeals for Veterans Claims has ruled in several cases that, if as a result of any treatment by the VA, a condition worsens, then the veteran is entitled to service connection for that condition.

Injury by medical staff in any VA facility can also be brought into federal court under tort statutes. Between June 1997 and December 1998 the VA staff made nearly three thousand medical mistakes, with seven hundred patient deaths resulting. You have the right to sue the VA hospital, doctors, or medical staff if your condition worsened as a result of negligence. However, you have only two years from the time of the alleged treatment to file an action against the VA in federal court. This type of action requires the services of an attorney.

These two types of actions against the VA are quite different. An 1151 claim requires only proof that your condition worsened as a result of VA treatment, whereas a lawsuit in federal court requires proof of negligence in order to prevail. If you are successful in federal court, you will receive the amount of your award for the injuries or health problem caused by the VA. However, if you filed a dual action against the VA (in other words, a claim for compensation or Dependency and Indemnity Compensation [**DIC**] benefits *and* a lawsuit in federal court), the VA will not pay compensation benefits until an amount equal to the lawsuit award has been matched by VA compensation benefits.

Keep in mind that before taking any kind of action, you must obtain a copy of all your hospital and outpatient medical records. You are entitled to copies of all medical records under the provisions of the Freedom of Information Act, and you do not have to justify your reason for requesting these records to a clerk.

Chapter 2 Highlights

The VA will deny any claim that does not meet the test of being well grounded. Unless the evidence is sufficient to convince a fair and impartial individual that the claim is plausible, the VA will not assist in the development of the claim. This chapter focuses on three important rules for making a claim.

First, service connection will be granted for preexisting medical conditions only if it can be shown that the condition was aggravated by conditions related to your military service. VA regulation 38 CFR §3.303(c) encourages the denial of any claim for a chronic condition that originated before entry into active duty. Therefore, for a claimant to prevail, the evidence must show that the condition worsened as a result of military service and is not the result of the natural progression of the disease.

Second, service connection is an uncomplicated process *if* your medical records are well documented and you file your claim immediately upon leaving the service or within one year following separation. Service connection can also be granted for medical conditions that become disabling beyond the one-year presumptive period if they manifest to a degree of 10 percent and have been identified as one of the presumptive diseases. Diseases associated with radiation exposure, Agent Orange, the Persian Gulf War, or being a POW; asbestosis, tropical diseases, and chronic diseases; and residual effects from voluntary or involuntary biochemical exposure fall under this liberalized rule. For the veteran who does not file a claim within the first year following separation or is not protected under one of the presumptive conditions, the evidence must show continuity of treatment from the time of separation to the date of the claim.

Third, establishing service connection to support a claim of poor treatment by VA hospitals or medical staff is detailed in Chapter 5. Every day veterans are finding themselves considerably more disabled as a result of treatment by VA staff or hospitals. It is becoming common to read or hear in the media that some veteran died or was seriously disabled as a result of treatment at a VA hospital.

As restrictive as these rules seem, service connection can be established if it can be proven that the condition claimed was caused by the aggravation of a preexisting condition or a chronic disease recognized under the presumptive rule, or if medical evidence establishes continuity of treatment. Service connection for treatment by the VA does not hinge only on negligent treatment.

Filing the Right Kind of Claim

The VA sorts all claim actions into one of six categories depending on the type of claim being submitted. However, only the first three groups of the six are covered in this book. The six primary groups are

- informal claim
- original claim
- reopened claim
- claim based on treatment by VA medical services
- amended claim
- claim based on secondary disabilities

It is extremely important for veterans to properly identify the type of claim action for the benefit they are seeking. Doing so will expedite the judicial review process if an appeal of the VA decision is necessary. It is equally important to prevent the VA from improperly identifying the purpose of the claim. For instance, if you want an increase for your disability because the condition has become more severe, you would *not* say, "I want to reopen my claim because my condition has become more severe." "Reopen" is jargon applying only to a claim that was previously denied and for which an appeal was not initiated. Instead, what you should say is, "My service-connected hearing condition has become more severe and I request to be reevaluated for increased benefits."

Informal Claim: The Anti-Denial Weapon

When putting together a winning claim, the proper use of an informal claim is one of the best tools a veteran has. It cannot be overemphasized that submitted claims must be complete and provable. Take time to develop evidence to support your contentions; you cannot afford to develop your claim by bits and pieces. The beauty of an informal claim is that the claim entitlement date is established and protected while you obtain evidence and necessary documents.

The governing regulation, 38 CFR §3.155, specifically defines an informal claim as any communication or action that indicates intent to apply for one or more benefits under the laws administered by the VA. Upon receipt of an informal claim, the VA must formalize the application by forwarding the appropriate form to the claimant. The official application (VA Form 21-526, Veteran's Application for Compensation and/or Pension) must be received by the VA within one year from the date it was mailed to the claimant for benefits to be granted based on the informal claim date.

Several other regulations call for specific action by the VA when an informal claim is filed. Under 38 CFR §3.150 ("Forms to Be Furnished"), the VA is required to provide the claimant with the appropriate application. Under 38 CFR §3.151, the claimant must file the specific form prescribed by the secretary in order for benefits to be paid. Next, the issue of how long the claimant has to file an application is spelled out in 38 CFR §3.109 ("Time Limit"). The provision 38 CFR §3.109(b) grants the VARO the authority to extend the one-year date if the claimant can show good cause for the delay in submitting the official application.

When veterans decide to file for VA benefits, they usually

call the VARO, which sends them an application. Veterans complete the form to the best of their ability and return it without any thought as to what they will need to prove the claim. The natural assumption is that the VA will get the evidence that is necessary to grant the benefits.

However, when the claimant is notified that the claim is not well grounded, and therefore denied, the first question that usually comes to mind is, "Why did they disapprove the claim when they know that I hurt my back on active duty? The pain and problems I have today are directly related to that injury!" At this point, the claimant is in a defensive position. With persistence, he may eventually succeed. However, it may take several years and maybe a trip or two to the BVA before benefits are granted.

Anytime you are planning to file a claim, the first thing you should do is file an informal claim. An informal claim is no more than a written notice of intent to file a claim for benefits. Look at this example:

> Please accept this notice as my informal claim for com-
> pensation benefits due to a back injury I had while on
> active duty in 1967. I have been treated for this condition
> at the VA hospitals in Lake City, Florida, in 1968; Hous-
> ton, Texas, in 1973; and The Bronx, New York, in 1980.
> A formal application will be filed once I have collected all
> the evidence to support my claim for disability benefits.

This simple notice has one other lasting benefit—it gives you the grounds for an appeal if benefits are denied. By regula-tion, under the "Duty to Assist" rule, and by several decisions by the United States Court of Appeals for Veterans Claims, the VA must get the required records once it has been advised that they exist. If the VA fails to do so, it most likely will deny the claim, and after you appeal, the BVA would vacate the decision and remand the case to the VARO for readjudication after the records have been obtained.

This notice can be submitted on VA Form 21-4138, Statement in Support of Claim, or in a personal letter to the VARO. Make sure you have a copy of everything you send the VA, including letters, documents, forms, and medical records. Deliver the application package to the VARO if possible. When you turn over the package, have the application and all attached evidence date-stamped. Then have them photocopy the application and all attachments for your personal records. Should it be necessary to mail your claim and evidence to the VA, send it by certified mail, return receipt requested. Do this whenever you correspond with the VA by mail. (See chapter 8.) I know of many veterans who lost thousands of dollars because they failed to take this one step. The VA lost their informal claim, and they could not prove they filed at an earlier date.

Formal Claims: Choosing the Right One

Most claim actions fall under the category of "new claims." By VA definition, a new claim generally involves a review of new evidence based on a new application. The VA separates new claim requests into the following groups:

- original claim
- amending an original claim
- claim for increased benefits
- total disability based on individual unemployability
- special compensation claim
- claim for posttraumatic stress disorder
- claim for a complication or injury resulting from medical treatment by VA medical services

- claim for adjunct disabilities
- claim based on presumptive diseases
- claim for pensions
- burial benefits

Only original claims, amending an original claim, claims for increased benefits, and claims for a complication or injury resulting from treatment by VA medical services will be detailed in this book.

A new claim is one in which the claim was never previously decided and the evidence is new and material (relevant) to the claim. The decision to either grant or deny the claim is based on current medical evidence and not on medical evidence used to decide an earlier claim.

To illustrate this point, let us say our claimant is a former POW who was previously denied service connection for arthritis resulting from being beaten with a rifle butt. Because there was no evidence in the file supporting his alleged injuries, the claim was initially denied. Later, the law was changed: if a POW was diagnosed as having arthritis, disabling to a degree of 10 percent, it was presumed to be service connected. This time, the veteran goes back to the VA with proof he was a POW. Because of the presumptive rule, the claim will now be considered a new claim for service connection, and the new medical evidence confirming the existence of arthritis will be used to decide the claim. The earlier evidence in his file will not be considered in the decision process.

ORIGINAL CLAIM

By definition, an original claim is the first claim filed for a particular benefit. It must be a first-time claim for service connection for a particular disease or injury as distinguished from a subsequent claim to reopen. The court has held that an original claim must be well grounded before the VA has a statutory duty to assist the veteran during the nonadversarial process of claims adjudication. In *Murphy v. Derwinski, 1 Vet. App. 78 (1990)*, the court ruled, "The initial burden to justify a belief a claim is well grounded is *on the shoulders of veteran or claimant* [emphasis added]." The ruling in this case defined a "well-grounded claim" as a plausible claim, one which is meritorious on its own or capable of substantiation. Such claims need not be conclusive but only possible to satisfy the initial burden of the statute (Title 38 United States Code Annotated (U.S.C.A.) §5107(a)) to show the claim is well grounded. (This complex rule is discussed separately in Chapter 9.)

The only acceptable form to use to apply for original compensation benefits is Form 21-526, Veteran's Application for Compensation and/or Pension. Wartime veterans who wish to apply for pension benefits must also use this multipurpose form. (Pension benefits and pertinent information necessary to file a pension claim are not discussed in this book.)

The key to minimizing a processing delay with your application is to provide all required information. If you are filing a claim for compensation benefits for an injury or disease that occurred in the service, you must follow certain rules. First, because this is a multipurpose form, certain parts are not applicable to compensation. Further, by providing unnecessary information about yourself and your family, you reveal information that otherwise would not be available to this or any other agency. Right now, the Privacy Act provides some protection against making information available to a third party. However, your life could get very complicated very quickly should Congress allow this agency to furnish others with all of the information it has about you. However, if you are requested to provide information in a certain section, make certain that you answer the questions completely. *Do not* provide partial answers, as your claim will be returned with a request for full disclosure. Only three parts (A, B, & C) of the four-part VA Form 21-526 (revised August 2001) applies to compensation benefits:

Part A:

Section I: Type of claim being filed (items 1 through 2b)

Section II: Identification information (items 3 through 13d)

Section III: Active duty information (items 14 through 17d)

Section IV: Reserve duty (items 18a through 18p)

Section V: National Guard duty (items 19a through 19n)

Section VI: Travel information (items 20a through 20e)

Section VII: Military benefits in receipt of (items 21a through 21f)

Section VIII: Direct deposit information (items 22 through 24)

Section IX: Remarks

Part B.

Section I: About disability claimed (items 1 through 4b)

Section II: Disabilities due to exposure (items 5a through 10c)

Section III: Remarks (item 11)

Part C:

Section I: Dependency (items 1 through 12e)

Section II: Previous marriages (items 13a through 14g)

Section III: Information about dependents (items 15 through 21f)

VA Form 21-526: Giving the Right Answers

Completing a detailed form yet not knowing why certain information is required can be a nightmare. What happens if I don't

know what answer to give? Do they just want the year when
they ask for a date or must I cite the day, month, and year?
So it goes, line by line and page by page. What do I do when
there is not enough space for an answer? I don't understand
some of the questions—now what do I do?

On the other hand, you don't want to supply too much
information. Since VA Form 21-526 is a multipurpose form
shared with applications for pension benefits, it requests information regarding personal finances that is not applicable for a
compensation claim. It is none of the VA's business how much
you earn, what you invest in, or what your monthly ex-
penses are.

Section II: Identification   The first section is a group of questions that provide the VA with sufficient background information to track you. If you ever served under a different name,
make certain this information is entered in item 1c. After leaving
the service you may have changed your name, whether because
of **marriage** or other reasons. To ensure that military records
pertaining to you are located, enter your complete name as it
was recorded on all documents from the time you entered
service until you were separated. Without this information, the
VA will not be able to obtain your military records from any
of the NPRC storage sites.

On the application, items 3a and 13d must be answered, as
required by statute. If you are married and do not report your
spouse's or children's (item 6 in Part C, Section I) social
security numbers, the claim will not be processed until that
information is provided. If an eight-digit VA claim number
was never assigned, the VA will most likely assign your social
security number and preface it with CSS-. If you have been
assigned a "C" number, enter it in Part A, Section X, item 29.

If you ever filed any kind of action with the VA, write in Section X, item 29, the regional office that processed your claim action.

Section III: Service Information   For each period of service, you must provide complete and accurate information. You must include a certified copy of your DD-214 or Report of Separation for each period of service. The application states, "Attach DD-214 or other Report of Separation (original) to expedite the processing of your claim." It is not wise to send the VA your original document because it can be easily lost. The VA will accept a copy of your separation documents if the original is recorded and certified by the clerk of the court in the county where you live. If you have lost your original document, you can obtain a certified copy from the NPRC by submitting a Standard Form (SF) 180. Once you receive the document or documents from the NPRC, take them to the courthouse, have them recorded, and obtain certified copies to attach to your application.

Sections IV and V: Active, Reserve, and National Guard Service   This section has two main objectives. For members of a federal military reserve organization or National Guard who were disabled because of duties, Part B, Sections I & II address possible VA entitlement to benefits. The second purpose is to determine how disability severance pay, downsizing pay, or military retirement pay may affect possible VA benefits.

If the claimant ever served in a reserve or National Guard unit or retired from the active duty, this is an important section. If he joined one of these units after leaving the active service, pertinent records that were part of his active duty file may have been transferred to one of these units. These records are not archived in the same place or under the same system as active duty records. If you are looking for documents to substantiate your claim, knowing where to go and what to ask for may be the difference between having your claim approved and having it denied. Also, any time you are injured during a scheduled reserve drill period you are entitled to compensation benefits. On the other hand, the only time members of a state National Guard unit are eligible for VA benefits is if they were injured when their unit was activated into federal service.

Part A, Section VII, items 21a–21e seek information concerning military retirement pay. The VA is prohibited by statute from paying a disabled retired veteran compensation benefits if the veteran is receiving full retirement pay. You should elect to accept VA compensation benefits in part because what you receive from the VA is tax-free income. The combined amount received from the VA and the reduced retirement pay from the service still equals your gross military retirement benefit. You simply get two checks each month instead of just one.

The size of the disability severance pay, Section VII, item 21f, awarded when you separated from the service will determine how long you will have to wait for the VA to start compensation payments. The law requires the VA to offset an amount equal to the amount of severance pay. It is to your advantage to file immediately for compensation benefits upon separation, as it will start the countdown clock before benefits can be paid. On the other hand, if you waited five years before filing, then the VA will start withholding compensation benefits five years after you left the service. The loss of benefits can be considerable. There is also the danger that if you wait past the presumptive period, the VA will make you show continuity of treatment before benefits are granted.

Item 21f addresses monies veterans receive as lump sum readjustment pay or for separation from the service. Active duty personnel are separated because it is a politically feasible way to gain favor with some of the voters by reducing the budget and reducing taxes. The veteran caught in this situation is a victim of the same game plan large corporations use to cut overhead and increase net profit. Congress wrote into the law that if a veteran is in receipt of lump sum readjustment pay, the VA is required to withhold payment of any compensation benefits that might become due until an amount equal to the severance pay is withheld. In other words, a veteran cannot receive both severance pay and compensation benefits at the same time. This is without doubt one of the most unjust acts Congress ever passed regarding the citizens who have served this country.

If a veteran should discover that he is medically incapacitated by a presumptive disease many years after leaving the service and receiving severance pay, the VA cannot start paying compensation for the illness incurred in the service until a like sum is withheld.

Part B, Section I: Nature and History of Disabilities   There is not much space in item 11 to describe and date all the conditions for which service connection is being claimed. VA regulations and several court decisions dictate that when a veteran files a claim for service connection, the regional office rating boards are required to examine all the military medical records and rate all conditions they found in the service file whether or not the veteran claimed the condition. Service connection is to be granted for any condition identified in 38 CFR Part 4. However, what they are supposed to do and what they actually do are seldom the same, for many reasons.

For starters, rating boards are no longer composed of a doctor, attorney, and rating specialist. Single board members rate all types of claims and make technical medical decisions without benefit of medical training and experience. No doctors, attorneys, or paralegals take part in the decisionmaking process. To further complicate and deteriorate the adjudication process, the VA made a change to VA Manual M-21, Part VI, Chapter 1, that will allow a rating board member to accept the medical thoroughness of an examination by nurse practitioners or physician's assistants in deciding the merits of a claim.[1]

The disservice of this type of operation can easily be equated to the problems being identified in health maintenance organizations (HMOs), where individual healthcare is actually determined by nonphysicians. Both Congress and VA bureaucrats are looking at the expense sheet when deciding policy. They have no medical experience and no concern for the patient. Every legitimate claim turned down is money the VA does not have to spend.

If you are claiming more than one or two conditions, you need to write "See attached sheet detailing the medical conditions that I am claiming. I request that my file be reviewed in its entirety and service connection granted for all medical problems I may not have identified" in item 17. When listing the claimed conditions, make certain each is assigned a number.

---

[1] When you are scheduled for a Compensation & Pension Examination always ask the examiner what his medical specialty is and if, in fact, he is a medical doctor. An unqualified examiner is sufficient ground for the basis of an appeal if your claim is denied or not rated at the level of your true disability.

When the VA returns its decision establishing service connection and fails to consider every item claimed, you have grounds for an appeal.

If the information requested in any items is not applicable, enter "N/A" in each box. You want to make certain the VA understands that you looked at the information requested but decided it does not apply to your claim. You want to make certain that the VA has no reason to return your claim for additional information or confirmation of the facts, thus delaying the claim process by several months.

Part B, Section I, items 1 through 4b establish who treated you, and when and where you were treated for the conditions being claimed. Items 3 and 4 will give the VA a starting point for where to look for medical records. A veteran who served 5, 10, 15, 20, or more years will have been treated for medical problems at many military installations.

Again, the space is not adequate to accommodate the information requested. Attach a separate sheet of paper using the format outline in item 1 to record your answers. Remember that outpatient records stay with an individual throughout his entire period of service. However, if a veteran is hospitalized in a military hospital, those records stay with the hospital and do not follow him to his next duty station. When hospital records are retired to the NPRC, they are stored in a location designated for hospital records. They are not filed with the military file or outpatient records.

Part B, Section I needs to be answered with great clarity. This medical information concerning your condition can have a major bearing on how your claim will be decided. Lay evidence and the importance of obtaining acceptable admissible medical evidence will be discussed in chapter 6.

If you are going to attach a separate sheet to report all the information requested in items 1 through 6, make certain you inform the VA of this by adding this remark to each relevant section on the application: "See attached sheet for complete information pertaining to this section."

Complete VA Form 21-4142, Authorization and Consent to Release Information to the Department of Veterans Affairs, for each private physician or hospital that can provide copies of medical records pertinent to your claim. Obtaining and packaging medical evidence to support your claim will be discussed in detail in chapter 8.

Marital and Dependency Information   In Part C, Section I, items 1 through 12, the VA is soliciting detailed information concerning your current marriage and all previous marriages for yourself and your spouse. They also want to know certain basic facts about your children. There are several reasons for requesting this information. For instance, if you are rated 30 percent or more disabled and have dependents, you will receive an additional monetary benefit. The dollar amount of this additional benefit depends on the number of dependents you have and to what degree you are disabled. Make certain that you answer every question. If there is no answer for a particular box, write "N/A" so the VA knows you did not overlook the question. Most important, when the VA asks for information concerning all marriages, present or past, and how each marriage was terminated, make certain that you give complete answers. For example, for date and place of marriage don't write "Texas 1952." The correct way to report this information is "Lubbock, Texas, June 3, 1952." The same rule applies for information concerning the termination of a marriage. The information must be very accurate; the VA may decide to verify this information with the agency responsible for archiving the documents. Failure to provide complete information will delay your claim or extra benefits until proof is provided. Currently, the VA is supposed to accept your word concerning marital information. However, it would be prudent to attach a copy of the documents to the application. If you do not have the documents, try to obtain a copy before you file your application for benefits. (Documents and their importance are discussed in chapter 7.)

Remarks In the Remarks block (item 29), tell the VA what you are claiming and how many extra sheets containing detailed information are attached. For example, "This is a claim for compensation benefits. Four pages of detailed information are attached." The space provided for "Remarks" is inadequate to detail the facts of your claim. To ensure that there is a detailed account of your claim, prepare VA Form 21-4138, Statement in Support of Claim, as an addendum to the original claim.[2]

AMENDING AN ORIGINAL CLAIM

When you want to add to the list of injuries or diseases claimed in your original application, you are filing what is known as an amended claim for injuries or diseases that occurred in the service. You do not submit a second original claim on VA Form 21-526 for these medical problems. It is preferable to submit your claim on VA Form 21-4138, Statement in Support of Claim, rather than stating the request in a personal letter. The

---

[2] See this chapter and chapters 4 and 5 for examples of VA Form 21-4138 contents detailing the disability you are claiming.

statement requesting service connection for these additional injuries or diseases should be simple and to the point.

The same rules for supporting an original claim apply to the amended claim. The evidence must show that you did in fact suffer from an injury or disease on active duty. If you are going to amend your claim, do so within the first year after leaving the service. Once the one-year presumptive period passes, the burden is on you to submit a well-grounded claim and show continuity of treatment for the conditions claimed. As previously mentioned, continuity of treatment means being able to show a clear and continuous treatment for the condition since leaving the service. The longer you wait to file a claim, the greater the risk of your request being initially denied.

Your statement should read something like this in order to trigger the VA's duty to assist:

I request to amend my original claim for service con-nected disabilities submitted on January 3, 1990, to in-clude a right leg injury resulting from a through-and-through gunshot wound. It was one of the seven wounds I received while on patrol north of Da Nang, Vietnam, in 1972. I was treated by a field medical unit, and then transferred to the Air Force hospital at Cam Ranh Bay, Vietnam. Following surgery I was air evacuated to the naval hospital in San Diego, California, where I was an inpatient for six months. I was rated 20 percent disabled by a Navy and Marine Corps Physical Evaluation Board for the residuals of wounds to my upper left arm and chest and subsequently given a medical discharge with severance pay. Attached is a letter from Doctor Howard Roberts, confirming that the wound to my right leg is a through-and-through gunshot wound. Dr. Roberts has been treating me for chronic pain and loss of mobility for the past five years because of the damage the shell fragments caused as they passed through my leg muscles. Attached is my wife's sworn statement describing the decreasing physical ability she has observed as a result of my right leg wound. Her testimony covers the observations she made during the fifteen years of our marriage.

The information in this statement gives the claimant considerably more control over how the VA will initially rate this claim for additional benefits. The claimant has informed the VA that he was wounded in combat, that his wound was through and through, where he was hospitalized, and for how long. The medical records attached show the claimant was under a doctor's care for pain and loss of mobility that were directly related to the gunshot wound. The sworn statement given by the claimant's wife describing her husband's declining physical condition during the years of their marriage as a result of the right leg wound provides lay evidence the VA must accept and weigh with the medical evidence provided by his doctor.

The VA must accept the claim as being well grounded because it happened during combat operation. It has to rate the claim under 38 CFR §4.71. Depending upon which muscle group is involved, the minimum rating would be between 10 and 20 percent. Next, the VA has to consider the additional complication of chronic pain and lost mobility in arriving at a final rating. Because the claimant provided medical and lay evidence to support the claim, the rating board must order a C&P Examination. If the board is inclined to grant the minimum rating, it must detail why it rebutted your physician's findings and what evidence it has that is superior to the evidence you provided that led to this decision. This example also opens the door to possible retroactive benefits because the VA has a duty to rate all disabilities the claimant may have regardless of whether they were specified.

CLAIM FOR INCREASED BENEFITS

A claim for increased benefits is one of the most dangerous claim actions a veteran can file. You think that your service-connected medical condition has increased in its severity, so you decide to file a claim for increased benefits. A majority of veterans base this decision on what they perceive as a deterioration of their health problem without a current medical assessment from their physician as to the actual degree of disability involved. Seldom will a veteran discuss the current level of his disability with a private physician before filing a claim for increased benefits. It is also true that the average veteran will not determine exactly what he must medically prove before filing a claim for increased benefits.

With few exceptions, a veteran has no idea what the VA's requirements are to increase a disability rating to the next rating level. In most cases, a veteran files a claim for increased disability benefits without any knowledge of how the VA rates claims for increased benefits. In many cases, the claimant ends up having his benefits confirmed at the current level, reduced to a lower percentage, or terminated. If the veteran wishes to challenge the decision, a Notice of Disagreement must be filed in order to start the appeal process. It will be three to five years before the matter is finally settled. Unless the veteran is fortunate enough to find professional assistance in dealing with the issues on appeal, the chance of restoring his benefits is slim.

There is a way to improve the odds when filing a claim for increased benefits. First, you must know the exact rating code your disability is classified under. To do this you must obtain a complete copy of your claim file. You are entitled by law to complete copies of all the files the VA has on you. Once you have a copy of your claim file, find the most recent rating decision and determine the four-digit rating code assigned to your disability.

The next step is to go to your local law library and find the rating code number assigned to your disability in 38 CFR Part 4. Photocopy this page of the regulation so you will have it for your doctor. To give you an idea of what to look for, let's use the example of a lumbosacral strain identified as rating code number 5295. The maximum rating that can be granted for this type of lower back injury is 40 percent. The criteria for each degree follow:

- "Severe; with listing of whole spine to opposite side, positive Goldthwaite's sign, marked limitations of forward bending in standing position, loss of lateral motion with osteoarthritic changes or narrowing or irregularity of joint space or some of the above with abnormal mobility on forced motion": 40% rating
- "With muscle spasm on extreme forward bending, loss of lateral spine motion, unilateral, in standing position": 20% rating
- "With characteristic pain on motion": 10% rating
- "With slight subjective symptoms only": 0% rating

If you were currently rated 10 percent for a lumbosacral strain, to be eligible for an increase you would have to show medically that your current level of disability is as described for a higher rating. Provide your doctor with this information and request a letter from him describing your current level of disability, using VA standards.

The last step before filing a claim is to compose a statement on VA Form 21-4138 stating your intent. Again, the statement should be short and to the point, covering the technical requirements of your claim. I would suggest something along these lines:

> Please accept this statement as a request for increased benefits for my service-connected lower back injury rated under rating code 5295. My orthopedic physician, Dr. Robert Young, after reviewing VA standards for a lumbosacral strain, finds that my condition is best rated under "severe at 40%." His letter of April 1, 1997, details his medical findings. Also enclosed is a sworn statement from my wife of twenty years whose lay observations report the difficulty I have in dealing with everyday tasks due to pain and loss of motion.

Once again, you have taken the initiative by backing your claim with hard medical evidence. To dispute this claim, the VA must show that its evidence is superior to your specialist's evaluation and that the preponderance of evidence is against the claim. In not granting the 40 percent rating, the VA must provide you with the evidence that required the denial of your claim for increased benefits. The VA's letter to you cannot be vague or generalized. Here again you are in a good position to challenge the decision on appeal.

The law provides a safety net to protect a veteran who has been rated for a condition for twenty or more years. 38 CFR §3.951(b) states that once a condition has been rated at the same level for twenty or more years, the rating cannot be reduced except in the case of fraud. The twenty-year period is computed from the effective date of the evaluation to the effective date of reduction of evaluation. Beware that the VA has been known to target 100-percent-rated individuals for periodic C&P Examinations within six months of the twenty-year time frame as a culling process. Usually the individual is ill prepared to cope with a reevaluation, which results in the rating being reduced. Keep records of doctors who have treated you for your condition. If you are changing doctors or moving, ask for copies of your records.

There is protection against a 100 percent rating being reduced when the rating has been in force for five or more years. This regulation, 38 CFR §3.343(a), requires the VA to show a material improvement in the veteran's condition over the examination and evaluation that granted the initial 100 percent rating. The court further enforced this provision when deciding *Karnas v. Derwinski, 1 Vet. App. 308 (1991)*. The court ruled the VA could not reduce a total rating unless it can prove the condition has actually improved. A great deal is at stake when the VA reduces a 100 percent rating to a lesser rating. It could mean losing $1,000 or more a month in monthly benefits. If you are notified of a reduction and your condition has not improved, file a Notice of Disagreement to protect your rights and find a competent service officer to assist you in the appeal process.

Chapter 3 Highlights

The surest way to a great deal of grief is to ask for the wrong benefit. Improperly identifying your claim will generate considerable delays before a decision is rendered. Anytime the VA sends a letter requesting additional information or clarification of facts, two to three months are added to the processing time. Asking to *reopen* your claim, for instance, when you actually need to *amend* the original claim can bring about a denial of benefits. The statutes require all claims to be submitted on the proper form. Failure to file the correct form will cause delays in processing and/or denial of benefits.

An *informal claim* is one of the best tools a veteran has. Intent is immediately made known and the effective date of the benefit is established. The VA cannot start the adjudication process until the formal application is filed. The VA is required by statute to send you the correct application form for the benefit being claimed when you file an informal claim. You have one year from the date the official application is mailed to you to file the claim. Benefits are retroactively adjusted to the date your informal claim was date-stamped into the VA. Make certain that you follow the instructions detailed in this chapter when submitting your informal claim. Do not be one of the people who lose thousands of dollars because they cannot prove they filed an informal claim.

Within the *New Claim* category are four separate claim actions. In view of their individual importance, a separate chapter is designated for each. By definition, a new claim action is one in which the claim was never previously decided and the evidence is new and material to the claim.

A claim for compensation or pension benefits is submitted on VA Form 21-526 and must accurately reflect all the information necessary to permit a **determination** of benefits. Only those items discussed above are required to be completed when the claim is for compensation benefits. In all sections where you are not required to provide information, write "N/A" in big block letters. Answer every required question accurately. Do not give incomplete answers. In a separate statement (use VA Form 21-4138) attached to the application, detail the circumstances and facts of each injury or disease being claimed. The minimum information that should be provided includes when and where the medical problem occurred; details of treatment history; whether the injury or disease was combat related; and how the condition affects your work and social adaptability. Last, make certain that you have a complete copy of the application and all attached documents for your personal file. The burden is always on you to prove you filed a claim for benefits and submitted evidence to substantiate that claim. (The correct way to substantiate and file a claim is discussed in chapters 7 and 8.)

Amending an original claim is nothing more than adding additional injuries or diseases to the original claim. Because the amended claim is an addition to the original claim, you do not have to meet the well-grounded test before the VA will rate the claim based on the evidence of record or the new evidence you submitted. The VA is bound by statute to rate all service-incurred disabilities even though the veteran might not have specifically claimed them. In *Fanning v. Brown, 4 Vet. App. 225 (1993)* the court held that the "VA could not ignore or disregard a claim merely because the veteran did not expressly raise appropriate legal provisions which correspond to benefits sought." If the evidence was in the file, the veteran can request a retroactive adjustment of benefits if the VA failed to rate an injury or disease when the original claim was rated.

4 | CLAIMS BASED ON TREATMENT BY THE VA

Doing Things Our Way

The history of this benefit goes back more than seventy years to the passage of the World War Veterans' Act of 1924 when Congress extended service-connected benefits to any veteran who suffered a further injury or disability while hospitalized by the VA. The statute, known as "Section 213 Benefits," entitled a veteran to compensation benefits whether or not the injury or disability was the result of negligence by hospital staff.

A decade later, in 1934, the VA changed the regulatory language of the implementing regulation, making benefits payable only when negligence could be proven. Congress did not amend the law in 1934 to narrow the rights of a veteran who claimed additional injuries or disabilities while being treated by the VA. The VA undertook this initiative on its own. It was never Congress's intent to place on veterans the difficult burden of proving negligence in order to receive compensation.

For the next sixty years, the VA paid benefits only when a veteran could prove negligence was the cause of his disabilities. Over that time, veterans who suffered injuries or disabilities while being treated by the VA were deprived of lawfully entitled compensation benefits. There is no telling how many veterans were denied service connection—thousands or even tens of thousands—until a veteran by the name of Fred P. Gardner refused to accept the VA rationale.

Mr. Gardner filed a claim in November 1988 because an operation on his lower spine in 1986 was the direct cause of nerve and muscle damage to his left leg. The VARO denied his claim on January 26, 1989, on the basis that 38 CFR §3.358(c)(3) requires the disability to be the product of an accident or mistake by the VA medical staff. The VA maintained that there was no proof of negligence or accident regarding the medical procedure performed on his spine by VA hospital medical staff. The veteran filed a timely Notice of Disagreement with this decision and the VARO of original jurisdiction confirmed the denial of service connection in September 1989. A formal appeal was filed and forwarded to the BVA. The BVA reviewed the case in January 1990 and upheld the decision of the VARO. The BVA stated, "We do not find evidence of fault on the part of the VA or of the occurrence of an unforeseen, untoward event, resulting in permanent additional disability. Accordingly, entitlement to the benefits requested is not demonstrated."

Mr. Gardner filed a timely appeal to the United States Court of Appeals for Veterans Claims and his case was argued August 7, 1991. A favorable decision was rendered on November 25, 1991, as amended on December 3, 1991. The case, known as *Gardner v. Derwinski, 1 Vet. App. 584 (1991),* was almost as great a landmark decision as *Gilbert v. Derwinski, 1 Vet. App. 49 (1990).* This decision blasted a hole through the VA system of "Doing Things Our Way." The order read,

> The Court holds 38 CFR §3.358(c)(3) unlawful as exceeding the authority of the Secretary and in violation of the statutory rights granted to veterans by Congress

under section 1151. Accordingly, the decision of the BVA is REVERSED and the matter REMANDED for further proceedings.

Mr. Gardner won, but still waited another four years before the issue was finally closed. The VA did not give up its initiatives and power that easily. It appealed the decision of the United States Court of Appeals for Veterans Claims to the United States Court of Appeals for the Federal Circuit on March 9, 1992. The Federal Circuit issued its decision on September 13, 1993, upholding the United States Court of Appeals for Veterans Claims decision and affirmed the decision that 38 CFR §3.3 58(c)(3) was illegal. The order noted that "the VA's desire to pay less compensation than that authorized by statute could not make legitimate the unlawful nature of 38 CFR §3.358(c)(3). The VA must make its regulations carry out the purposes of a statute, not amend it." What's really interesting is one of the arguments raised by the VA to the Court of Appeals for the Federal Circuit. While the press releases were cranking out slogans about how much we owe our veterans, the secretary was in court arguing that acceptance of the VA's version of its regulation should prevail because of the cost of providing extra compensation to veterans who couldn't prove negligence or accident. If the decision of the United States Court of Appeals for Veterans Claims were upheld and the regulation invalidated, the VA would have to pay everybody whose physical condition was worse following treatment by the VA. The court told the VA, "[W]here a statute's meaning is clear, the cost of implementation is a concern for Congress, not the VA; the VA's duty is to pay benefits based on the clear language of the statute."

The secretary of the VA was determined to fight the loss

of a regulation that allowed it to save millions and millions of dollars. In January 1994, the solicitor general of the United States petitioned the U.S. Supreme Court on behalf of the VA to review the finding of the Court of Appeals for the Federal Circuit decision in *Brown v. Gardner 115 S Ct. 552, 13 OL Ed 2nd 462 (1994)*. The Supreme Court agreed to review the lower appeals court's findings. On December 12, 1994, the Supreme Court released its decision. It affirmed the lower court finding by a vote of 9 to 0. The Court held that the statute is quite clear and does not place any requirement on the veteran to show fault before compensation can be paid; and that just because the VA has been improperly applying the law for more than sixty years is not grounds to legitimize a regulation that contradicts the statute.

Eight years passed from the time Mr. Gardner filed his application for benefits to the time the Supreme Court decided that the VA illegally adjudicated his claim under a regulation that denied his right to benefits and contradicted the intent of Congress. During 1996, Mr. Gardner's victory on appeal will work its way back to the original VARO of jurisdiction to be readjudicated, this time based on the medical facts of his case. I have no information as to whether Mr. Gardner was granted service connection for the residual effects of his operation to the lower spine. If his claim was denied on different grounds, I imagine Mr. Gardner is once again fighting it out with the VA using the appeal system.

What the Regulations Say

The prevailing statute pertaining to an application for compensation benefits based on medical problems resulting from treatment by the VA medical system or health problems resulting from training under the Vocational Rehabilitation Program is 38 U.S.C. §1151, and the regulations implementing the statute arc 38 CFR §3.358(a)(b)(c) as revised and 38 CFR §3.800. The portion of the adjudication manual pertinent to an 1151 claim is M21-1 Part VI, Change 42, dated December 7, 1995.

Although the Supreme Court upheld the declaration of the United States Court of Appeals for the Federal Circuit and the United States Court of Appeals for Veterans Claims that proof of negligence was not the intent of Congress when it passed the World War Veterans Act of 1924, claims under 38 U.S.C. §1151 will always be difficult to win. The amended change to 38 CFR §3.358(c) leaves intact many of the original elements that a veteran must prove before entitlement is established.

For instance, the Supreme Court left intact the Doctrine of *Volenti non fit injuria*.[1] The decision also raised two other important elements a veteran must deal with in order to establish service connection. First, the Court held that 38 U.S.C. §1151 permits service connection for all but the *necessary consequences* of properly administered VA medical or surgical treatment or an examination to which a veteran consented.[2] The Court stated that compensation should not be payable for the necessary consequences of treatment to which the veteran consented. Claims will be adjudicated based on the interpretation that the meaning of "consent" applies to both expressed consent and implied consent.

---

[1] Blacks Law Dictionary defines *volenti non fit injuria* as knowing and comprehending the danger, voluntarily exposes him or herself to it, thought not negligent in so doing, he or she is deemed to have assumed the risk and is precluded from recovery for an injury resulting therefrom.

[2] A *necessary consequence* means those consequences certain or intended to result from treatment or examination.

The second element is informed consent, which is a major consideration when submitting a claim based on VA treatment. When undergoing a form of treatment or surgical procedure in a VAMC, you are required to give your consent for this treatment. It is the physician's responsibility to provide information related to your treatment and obtain your consent. He must record your consent in the "progress notes" section of your hospital record. If you consented to the treatment, you may not have a valid claim if the hospital staff followed the medical and administrative procedures exactly as published. The theory is that you acknowledged and accepted any risks.

The final rule change to 38 CFR §3.358(c) based on the Supreme Court decision in *Brown v. Gardner* was published in the *Federal Register* on May 23, 1996, and was amended as follows:

(3) Compensation is not payable for the necessary consequences of medical or surgical treatment or examination properly administered with the express or implied consent of the veteran or, in appropriate cases, the veteran's representative. *Necessary consequences* are those which are certain to result from, or were intended to result from, the examination, or medical or surgical treatment administered. Consequences otherwise certain or intended to result from a treatment will not be considered uncertain or unintended solely because it had not been determined at the time consent was given whether that treatment would in fact be administered.

What the rule does is narrow the VA's risk of being required to grant compensation benefits when the medical service provided may have an adverse affect. For example, suppose you gave permission for an exploratory surgical procedure for kidney problems. However, once your abdomen was opened, the exploratory procedure showed one kidney had to be removed. You cannot claim compensation benefits just because you now have only one kidney. Your kidney was removed because you gave implied consent. They were performing the procedure to determine the root of your medical problem. The permission to remove the kidney could also be justified if the doctor certifies that in his medical judgment, failure to remove the kidney might endanger your life.

The unchanged portions of 38 CFR §3.358(c) are key to determining whether your claim under 38 U.S.C. §1151 is compensable. To satisfy the requirements of conditions outlined in c-1 through c-7, the following conditions must be met:

- You have to show that the additional disability is actually the result of such disease or injury or an aggravation of an existing disease or injury and not merely a coincidence.
- You must be able to prove that the disease, injury, or aggravation of an existing condition was suffered as a result of VA medical or surgical treatment or hospitalization, or as a result of vocational rehabilitation training.
- You must be able to show that the injury or disease was not the result of your willful misconduct or failure to follow instructions. With the exception of incompetent veterans, veterans will be barred from compensation benefits if their conduct in any way led to complications related to their treatment.
- You must be able to prove that the disability you are claiming while in vocational rehabilitation training was directly caused by the activities involved in your training program.
- If you are injured or contract a disease while in a nursing

home under VA contract compensation, benefits under section 1151 are not payable. The VA holds that the nursing home is an independent contractor and, accordingly, is its own agent and its employees are not to be deemed employees of the VA.

A VA Tool to Skirt Entitlements

The requirement for a veteran to sign a consent statement and SF-522, Request for Administration of Anesthesia and for Performance of Operations and Other Procedures form before treatment is administered is a catch-22 situation. If you don't sign it, the VA sends you packing; if you do sign it, it can effectively insulate itself against granting service-connected benefits because you consented to the risks. So where does that leave veterans? You've got to know the rules the VA must follow.

Historically, the VA is known for not following its own laws, regulations, manuals, and policies. Following are what it must do when treating you:

- The doctor and only the doctor must inform you of the risks involved in the treatment that you are about to authorize. The physician must explain in detail the known consequences or expected consequences of the procedure you are to undergo. Possible consequences must also be discussed when the doctor knows the frequency of certain kinds of complications and there is a reasonable chance they could occur. Informed consent also means that the doctor discusses effects that are not intentionally caused, desired, or expected. It also means that alternative options are covered.
- The practitioner must document everything discussed in your inpatient medical record. The memo will include

the date and time the consent was given, your ability to comprehend the information (Were you awake and alert? Confused? Were you under some form of sedation at the time?), the fact that you were given an opportunity to ask questions, the fact that you gave your consent freely and were not under duress or coercion, and the fact that he discussed the medical treatment in understandable language.

- When a procedure entails use of sedation, produces considerable discomfort, has a risk of complications or death, requires injections of any substance into joint space or body cavity, and is classified as a surgical procedure, the VA *must* also obtain a signed SF-522. This release must also be made part of your inpatient hospital records.

Elements of an 1151 Claim

You may be entitled to compensation benefits based on disabilities resulting from treatment by VA medical staff or while in vocational rehabilitation. Your claim must be carefully crafted so that you can skirt limitations imposed by 38 CFR §3.358(a)(b)(c). Some special areas should be zeroed in on when determining if your claim has a chance of being granted. VA medical staff must fulfill specific responsibilities; otherwise, benefits must be granted. Failure of the VA to dot the i's or cross the t's is what to look for in developing evidence to justify the granting of benefits.

Service connection must be granted in the face of evidence of additional disability or death through carelessness, negligence, lack of proper skill, error in judgment, or similar instances of fault by VA healthcare providers. Benefits must also be granted if additional disability or death resulted from an accident that was not a reasonably foreseeable adverse event.

If procedures requiring signed consent do not show that the veteran was fully informed and that the claimed condition was a possible result of the medical procedure for which consent was given, then the claim must be granted. For example, suppose your doctor told you that if you consent to an operation, two conditions could occur. You grant your consent, but as a result of the operation you are now suffering from the complications of two conditions that were not discussed before the procedure. Your claim would have to be granted.

Another circumstance in which benefits would be granted involves fault by other than a VA medical staff member. Suppose your doctor prescribed a certain drug and you suffered a side effect causing an additional disability or even death. If it is determined that the pharmaceutical supplier filled the prescription incorrectly, you would be entitled to compensation.

When there is insufficient evidence to prove informed consent concerning a surgical procedure, other therapeutic treatment, or a prescribed course of treatment, the claim must be granted. Insufficient evidence in this category would include the hospital losing or failing to enter your informed consent in the records. The VA could also be challenged if someone other than your primary care physician, or the doctor doing the procedure, discussed the risks and possible complications associated with the procedure. *Only a doctor can review this information with you.*

Failure to properly diagnose or treat a condition can generate a claim based on acts of omission as well as acts of commission. VA policy establishes that a failure to diagnose in a timely manner or properly treat a symptom that directly causes increased disability or death may give rise to entitlement under section 1151. If a veteran is discharged prematurely from the hospital under the guidelines required by the hospital administrative process known as DRG (diagnostic related groups),[3] a possible claim action exists. Eligibility hinges on whether an early discharge caused a relapse or a worsening of the disability, or whether the timing of the discharge caused the disability to be aggravated beyond the level of natural progression associated with the condition.

Compensation is payable under section 1151 for any disability caused by medication that was prescribed by VA and taken or administered as prescribed, except for the necessary consequences associated with the disease. For example, if you were taking several medications and then given a drug that is known to cause kidney failure when interacting with those previously prescribed, you would have grounds for a claim.

Another area to look into is the professional skill level of VA physicians responsible for your treatment. The VA has extreme difficulty recruiting topflight medical specialists. I recall that one VA medical center used a nurse to function in the capacity of a gynecologist because none were on staff at the hospital. It is common practice to use part-time general practitioners and foreign doctors with minimal language skills to examine and treat veterans. In this hospital medical center, resident students from a local medical school work part-time to treat and examine veterans. Here lies an area of vulnerability for the VA medical system and the basis of a well-grounded

---

[3] To reduce the cost of hospitalization of Medicare patients, the government instituted the concept of DRG. It states that for any known condition there is a theoretical point at which the average patient can be released. Medicare pays the hospital for the number of days the DRG determined was maximum for the condition being treated. If the patient stays beyond this point the hospital cannot bill Medicare or the patient for the additional care. The VA adopted this concept in the late 1980s.

claim for the veteran. The statute states very clearly that if someone who lacks the proper skills treats you, you have the basis of a claim under section 1151. You can obtain the medical background of any doctor by contacting the American Medical Association (AMA), 515 N. State Street, Chicago, Illinois, 60610 (312-464-5000), and asking for the doctor's professional profile.

Filing an 1151 Claim

A claim for benefits for complications resulting from medical treatment by the VA, or for an injury or disease sustained while enrolled in a vocational rehabilitation training program, should be submitted on VA Form 21-4138, Statement in Support of Claim. The claim must be made in narrative form as there are no specific questions on the form.

If possible, type the narrative. The claim should be brief and the language carefully chosen, with your arguments based only on facts that can be supported by the evidence in your claim file and hospital records and the pertinent regulations that apply to your case.

It's important when basing your claim on disabilities arising from treatment by the VA that your claim statement shows your condition was not one that could have been anticipated or a necessary consequence of that treatment. You must scrutinize your records to ascertain exactly what consent you granted and whether the records show that you were (or were not) aware of the consequences of the intended treatment.

Before filing your claim, the first step is to obtain a complete copy of all your hospital records. These are the records you must get from the hospital in order to support your claim:

- the admission medical examination and history
- the operating report
- the discharge summary
- nursing notes
- lab test results
- X ray, MRI, and CAT scan summaries
- a complete list of all medication administered

These records are essential if you are trying to establish service connection under section 1151.

If you believe that the VA is responsible for your disability, the next step is to take these records to a medical specialist for review and confirmation that the treatment you received did in fact cause the disability you are claiming. Your doctor's written report must also address the issue of whether or not the disability incurred was normally a condition that could or would occur with the type of treatment administered.

At the same time you request hospital records, contact the VARO who is custodian of your VA claim file and request a complete copy of the claim file and vocational rehabilitation records. The VA cannot ignore this request—it is a right granted under the Freedom of Information Act. Most important, you want these records before you announce your intent to file a claim. Let me stress, you want these records before you file your claim. The success of your claim depends on the type of claim you put together. You have to know what you're talking about or you will lose.

Next, obtain a copy of the current Code of Federal Regulations (38 CFR) that is applicable to your claim. All VAROs are supposed to maintain a complete library of laws, regulations, VA circulars, manuals, and General Counsel opinions. If you can visit a VARO, do so and obtain a copy of every legal citation that is pertinent to your case. If travel to the VARO is not practical, consider contacting one of the service organizations that maintain full-time staff at every VARO such as the American Legion, Veterans of Foreign Wars, Disabled American Veterans, or the State Service Office. Tell them the citations you are looking for, and that you are preparing an 1151 claim and need to know exactly what laws, regulations, and manuals are currently in effect.

The claimant has the burden of submitting evidence sufficient to justify a belief by a fair and impartial individual that the claim is well grounded. A claim filed under section 1151 must meet this test. In *Murphy v. Derwinski, 1 Vet. App. 78 (1990)*, the court defined "well-grounded" as a "plausible claim, one which is meritorious on its own or capable of substantiation." In *Tirpak v. Derwinski, 2 Vet. App. 609 (1992)*, the court held that "Although the claim need not be conclusive, it must be accompanied by supporting evidence sufficient to justify a belief by a fair and impartial individual the claim is plausible." The court further clarified the meaning in *Grottveit v. Brown, 5 Vet. App. 91 (1993)*, in which it held that "where the determinative issue involves medical causation or medical diagnosis, competent medical evidence to the effect that the claim is 'plausible' or 'possible' is required." The bottom line is that without medical evidence to back your claim, you have no claim. A veteran's statement attesting to service connection is not sufficient to trigger the VA's duty to assist when the issue is a medical question of entitlement.

There is no statute of limitation in applying for service connection under this provision of the statute. You can still apply even if the treatment occurred fifty years ago. However, obtaining proof after such a long time could pose some difficulty. Remember, you have to be able to submit a well-grounded claim in order to have your claim adjudicated.

If the VA previously denied you benefits under section 1151 on the grounds that negligence was not shown, you may be entitled to benefits because the rule used to deny your claim was illegal. In this case, after you gather all of your evidence, reopen your claim based on a clear and unmistakable error.

Suing the VA in Federal Court

As a veteran or surviving spouse you can bring a civil suit against the Department of Veterans Affairs into federal court under the Federal Tort Claims Act for injuries or diseases resulting from medical malpractice. Actually, claims under 38 U.S.C. §1151 and the Federal Torts Claims Act can be filed at the same time if the basis of the claim is medical malpractice. The difference between these two remedies is that under section 1151, to recover for the disabilities resulting from treatment by the VA, you do not have to prove negligence. However, in federal court, recovery will hinge on establishing that disability or death was in fact the result of negligence.

If you prevail in federal court, any awards obtained under the Federal Torts Claims Act are offset by compensation benefits you might be entitled to or have received under section 1151. For example, say you are awarded $200,000 in federal court because of the disabilities incurred by the medical treatment by the VA, and are subsequently granted service connection at a rate of $2,000 per month. You would receive your first compensation check only after eight years and four months—the equivalent of $200,000.

If you are denied service connection on your case and you

win an appeal in federal court, you have grounds to reopen your claim based on new and material evidence. The legal and medical basis that succeeded in federal court would be the arguments used to establish service connection under section 1151.

To establish a claim in federal court, follow the basic steps outlined above in "Filing an 1151 Claim." Because this legal action is being decided in a court of law, you need to be represented by an attorney. Obtain the services of an attorney who specializes in medical malpractice cases and one who also practices in federal court. If you do not know such an attorney, contact the local bar association in your area and ask for a list of firms that specialize in medical malpractice cases.

I am not an attorney and therefore cannot go beyond this point in discussing the possibilities of action against the VA in federal court. I can, however, tell you that you have only two years from the date of the injury or within two years of the date the injury is discovered—whichever comes later—to bring suit under the Federal Tort Claims Act.

Chapter 4 Highlights

For more than sixty years the VA illegally adjudicated claims based on injuries or diseases resulting from treatment by the Department of Veterans Affairs. The Supreme Court ruled in *Brown v. Gardner* that a veteran or surviving spouse did not have to prove negligence before benefits could be granted based on treatment by the VA. The VA's action to change the statute's meaning by means of a regulation change was illegal. All prior decisions since 1934 in which benefits were denied because the claimant did not prove negligence can be reopened based on a clear and unmistakable error. The court decision changed only 38 CFR §3.358(c)(3), and left the remainder of the paragraph intact. One very important provision left intact was the Doctrine of *Volenti non fit injuria.*

This doctrine is now the VA's major tactic in justifying the denial of benefits because consent was given. Whether the consent was expressed or implied, it will be assumed that veterans knowingly and voluntarily exposed themselves to the dangers and risk of the treatment. Yet failure to consent to the prescribed treatment means the loss of medical treatment for the problem.

Remember, only the doctor can discuss the details of the treatment plan with you and ask for your permission. During this interview he must tell you what will occur, what to expect, possible secondary disabilities, and whether the treatment will correct the problem. If success is not completely assured, you must be advised of the percentage of success you could reasonably expect.

Do not sign any form or release unless a physician brings it to you. Demand that you be properly advised by a doctor, and not by a nurse, physician's assistant, social worker, or any other hospital staff member. As the VA employs the services of many foreign doctors, you may not understand what is being explained because of a language barrier. The VA still would be out of compliance with the regulations if it assigns such a physician because you must be able to comprehend the risks explained before you give your consent. Everything the attending physician discusses with you must be recorded in the progress notes. Your inpatient hospital records must also include a signed copy of your SF-522 if you are given anesthesia or undergo an operation or any other medical or surgical procedure. Failure of the VA to follow this procedure is basis for a well-grounded claim and the granting of benefits. If there is no proof that you were properly advised of the dangers involved, or if those records are missing, the VA must grant service connection for the disability claimed.

You must carefully screen all the records for evidence to establish the basis of a well-grounded claim. Even though you signed a consent or an SF-522, a claim can still be successfully argued if you can prove carelessness, negligence, lack of proper skill, error in judgment, an unforeseeable accident, an improper or delayed diagnosis, or authorized drugs that you are allergic to or that were in conflict with other medication being prescribed that resulted in additional disabilities or death.

Again, if you were not properly advised of the possible consequences of the treatment plan or if a hospital staff member other than your physician briefed you, you should file an 1151 claim. A premature discharge from the hospital resulting in medical complications that cause additional disabilities or aggravation of an existing condition is also grounds for a claim.

Taking the time to put together a well-organized claim is the only way of ensuring all the facts and evidence will be available to a rating board member. Do not assume that all you have to do is state that an event happened and the VA will jump in and build your case for you. The duty to assist comes into play only after the VA is convinced that the claim is well grounded. A well-grounded claim is one in which the evidence (medical and legal) allows an impartial individual to believe that there is a possibility of a claim.

Therefore, you must get copies of all pertinent medical evidence including hospital records, doctor's outpatient records, and assessments of your condition. You need a medical statement from your doctor confirming that the problem you are experiencing is definitely related to the VA treatment. The doctor must also state that the inpatient records show that you were not aware of the consequences of the treatment plan.

An individual who has no in-depth training in law or medicine is deciding your claim. Most likely he will rate the claim based only on personal instincts of what he perceives as the meaning of the medical or legal evidence. In addition, the great number of claims to be decided does not allow the luxury of researching facts or reading court decisions when determining each claim. There is no time to sift through several hundred pages of medical and legal evidence to determine if the claim is well grounded or the facts are sufficient to grant service connection based on the Doctrine of Reasonable Doubt. When a rating board member is uncertain as to what is actually involved, he will most likely deny the claim. If he errs, it will be in favor of the government. The unspoken motto of adjudication is *if the claimant does not agree with the decision, let him argue it out in the appeal system.*

If you suffered serious injury or death as a result of treatment by the VA, you or your surviving spouse should take all the medical records to an attorney specializing in medical malpractice to determine if you have a winnable case under the Federal Torts Claims Act. Remember, you have only two years from the date of injury or when you first discovered it to take action in federal court. Your evidence must be able to support a lawsuit that the VA was negligent in its treatment, and that your disability is the result of this treatment.

5 | CLAIMS BASED ON SECONDARY DISABILITIES

Why Should It Be So Difficult?

Secondary disability claims are straightforward and, if properly documented, should sail right through the adjudication process. What could be simpler? If your service-connected condition is the proximate cause for another medical problem, that condition also becomes service connected. Then why is this benefit one of the top five most difficult to establish?[1] One reason is directly related to local VARO rating board members and the other reason relates to the claimants. First, let's look at the VA. Within this group are several factors that account for the reason rating boards turn down many claims based on adjunct disabilities. Rating board members have difficulty in dealing with medical opinions. Medical opinions from fully qualified doctors or specialists are not treated as statements of factual medical evidence by many rating board members. I used to mutter bad words each time a well-documented claim based on adjunct disabilities was denied. Rating board members, who have vast discretionary powers to determine if the medical assessment by a specialist is a fact or conclusion, do so purely by speculation. These individuals, with no specialized

---

[1] The other four claims that are most difficult are original, reopened, amended, and service connection for treatment by VA medical services.

legal or medical training, most likely with only a high school diploma and maybe ten to fifteen years of VA service, are now sitting in this position of power. They reach deep into their pocket of "experience" and pull out a decision determining that the doctor doesn't know what he is talking about. Their "experience" tells them the claimant's doctor is offering a biased opinion.

A case in point was a veteran who was service connected for Buerger's disease. The condition eventually leads to arteriosclerosis obliterans heart disease, congestive heart failure, and severe ischemic cardiomyopathy. The veteran filed a claim to establish the advanced medical conditions as secondary to Buerger's disease in November 1988, and after several trips to the BVA was finally granted 100 percent service connection for these conditions in 1995. The first time the rating board denied the claim, the justification was based on the opinion of a part-time retired general practitioner employed by the VA who disputed the findings of the **appellant**'s non-VA cardiologist and the findings of another VA doctor.

The **Statement of the Case** rationalized that the relationship joining Buerger's disease and the other heart problems was a new, unsupported medical concept with no foundation. The rating board was provided with medical excerpts from a medical textbook, *A Primer of Cardiology,* written by a professor of cardiology at Tulane University in 1947, detailing the concept that the board member considered to be new. This medical publication—like the medical assessment by the veteran's doctor—did not alter the board member's decision. The claim made several trips to the BVA, and each time the case was remanded to the VARO to have a VA cardiologist examine the client. If you guessed that the same VA fee-basis doctor conducted the rescheduled C&P Examination, you're right. A notice was immediately served on the VARO indicating that the examination was flawed because it failed to follow the specific instruction of the remand order. By protesting, we got the appeal back on the waiting list to be returned to the BVA.

Finally the BVA took the decision away from the VARO and granted the benefits. The sad part is that the veteran lived only a little more than a year after the benefits were granted. How much better his life would have been if he had enjoyed seven years of benefits instead of seven years of aggravation.

The downsizing tactics used by the VA include enticing senior rating board members, authorizers, and section chiefs into early retirement. They are replaced with individuals with shallow experience. This movement to reorganize and reduce costs included eliminating the doctors assigned to each rating board. The "New VA," as it is now known, became well organized to deny thousands of claims because the frontline troops were inexperienced and untrained in medicine or law. The message being sent was "If you don't like our decision, appeal it."

The "New VA" was facing increased caseloads to be handled by less experienced decisionmakers. The next step was to alter the structure of rating boards. Three-member boards no longer evaluated claims. One-member boards were the new working tools of the VA. The grade levels of claims specialist were lowered to GS-9 and GS-11s. This new machine was whittling away the tremendous backlog of cases—but at the expense of the veteran.

Many veterans and service officers also added to the problem. Claims were filed with no factual evidence linking the service-connected condition to the alleged medical problems. Of the many appeals lost, the main reason was that the veteran did not prove the case. The veteran must submit a well-grounded claim. Perhaps thousands of individuals have conditions that could be service-connected, if they only knew how to prove their claim.

I'm probably going to say this several more times before the end of this book: Just because the VA has a duty to assist if the claim is well-grounded, *it does not mean you can rely on the VA to make your claim.* You must take the initiative; it is your responsibility to ensure that the claim you submit medically links your service-connected condition to the disabilities you are claiming as an adjunct condition.

Court Findings Related to Secondary Claims

Decisions by the United States Court of Appeals for Veterans Claims provide, so to speak, a list of dos and don'ts to be followed by both the VA and the veteran if a claim is to be satisfactorily adjudicated. Using these findings of the court and following the regulations greatly increases your chances of having benefits granted.

FOR THE VETERAN

- When an issue involves a determination based on medical etiology or medical diagnosis, competent medical evidence is required to fulfill a well-grounded claim. A belief by the claimant that his current condition is the result of his service-connected disability can and will be denied on the basis that the claim is not well-grounded if medical evidence is not the basis for the claim. *Lathan v. Brown, 4 Vet. App. 269 (1993)*
- The claimant must present a plausible claim, one which is meritorious on its own or capable of substantiation. *Murphy v. Derwinski, 1 Vet. App. 78 (1990)*

- The burden of submitting a well-grounded claim cannot be met merely by presenting lay testimony. A layperson cannot offer competent medical opinions. *Grottveit v. Brown, 5 Vet. App. 91 (1993)*
- A service-connected (including secondary service connection) claim must be accompanied by evidence that establishes that the claimant currently has the medical condition claimed. *Lynch v. Brown, 9 Vet. App. 456 (1996)*

FOR THE VA

- The VA cannot ignore a well-grounded claim by neglecting to address it or acknowledge it. *Travelstead v. Derwinski, 1 Vet. App. 344 (1991)*
- The VA cannot grant service connection when the claimant's service-connected condition aggravates, but is not the proximate cause of, a non-service-connected condition. *Leopoldo v. Brown, 4 Vet. App. 216 (1993)*
- The VA cannot make unsupported medical conclusions when justifying the denial of service connection. *Leopoldo v. Brown, 4 Vet. App. 216 (1993)*
- When the claimant presents a well-grounded claim, the VA has a duty to assist in developing the facts pertinent to the claim. *Murphy v. Derwinski, 1 Vet. App. 78 (1990)*
- The VA cannot ignore its own regulation about evidence of service connection; it is required to consider all the evidence of record, including medical records and all pertinent lay statements. *Harder v. Brown, 5 Vet. App. 183 (1993)*
- When a claim is denied, the rating board must state its reasons for doing so and, more important, point to a medical basis other than the board's own unsubstantiated opinion. *Paller v. Principi, 3 Vet. App. 535 (1992)*

Filing a Claim for Secondary Benefits

A claim for benefits resulting from medical disabilities secondary to a service-connected injury or disease should be filed on
VA Form 21-4138, Statement in Support of Claim. There is
no set format or a form that asks specific questions. The claim
is in narrative form and should be typed so that there can be
no misunderstanding as to what you are saying. The claim
should be brief and the language should be very carefully
chosen with arguments based only on the facts that can be
supported by evidence that relates the medical condition to
your service-connected disability.

The evidence should include an evaluation by a specialist
who will state that the disability claimed is linked to your
service-connected condition. The evidence should also include
copies of all relevant inpatient and outpatient treatment records.
The medical evidence must also show that you are currently
suffering from this claimed condition and the degree to which
it is disabling based on VA standards as outlined in 38 CFR
Part 4.

Before filing your claim, obtain a complete copy of all
pertinent medical and hospital records. Evidence in this category includes

- hospital admission medical examination and history report
- the operating report
- the discharge summary
- nursing notes
- lab test results
- X ray, MRI, and CAT scan summaries
- complete list of all medications administered

These records are essential when trying to establish service connection for a condition that is secondary to your service-connected disability.

While you are requesting non-VA hospital records, also request the VARO custodian of your VA claim file to provide a complete copy of the claim file. Your request for these records cannot be denied, nor can it be ignored by the VA. This is a right granted under the Freedom of Information Act. Most important, you want these records before you actually file a claim. Again, let me stress, *you want these records before you file your claim.* By reviewing your claim file, you can quickly determine if the VA has all your inpatient and outpatient military health records. If you were hospitalized on active duty, your hospital records will be filed under the treating hospital at the NPRC. To obtain a copy of these records you must make a separate request, one that is not part of a request for outpatient records.

The success of your claim depends on the type of claim you assemble. The effort you put into preparing the claim is directly proportional to what you get out of it. You have to know what you are talking about and what you can prove, or you lose.

Next, obtain a copy of the parts of the current Code of Federal Regulations (38 CFR Parts 3 and 4) that are applicable to your claim. All VAROs are supposed to maintain a complete historical library of laws, regulations, VA circulars, manuals, and General Counsel opinions. Visit the VARO, if possible, and obtain a copy of every legal citation that is pertinent to your case. If travel to the VARO is not practical, consider contacting one of the service organizations that maintain full-time staff at every VARO, such as The American Legion,

Veterans of Foreign Wars, Disabled American Veterans, or the State Service Office. Tell them what citations you are looking for and that you are preparing a claim based on medical problems secondary to your service-connected disability. Emphasize that you need to know *exactly* what laws, regulations, manuals, and so on are currently in effect and what they require in order to file a well-grounded claim. Do not accept a condensed verbal summary from the service officer over the phone. You need to read these published rules and regulations to properly prepare your claim.

The burden of submitting evidence sufficient to justify a belief by a fair and impartial individual that the claim is well grounded rests with you, the claimant. A claim for establishing medical conditions secondary to the original service-connected condition must meet this test. The bottom line is that without medical evidence, you have no claim.

A veteran's statement attesting to service connection is not sufficient to trigger the VA's duty to assist when the issue is a medical question of entitlement. Without a well-documented claim with strong supporting medical evidence, you will not be in control. When your claim proves entitlement based on VA regulations and standards, the VARO must dispute your evidence with more than just its own unsubstantiated opinion. The burden then rests on the VARO to prove that you're not entitled.

Your primary objective is to ensure that benefits are granted at the local VARO level without having to appeal. But, if you do appeal, you will win. It is a sorry state of affairs when the lowest level of a government agency makes it necessary for the claimant to turn to a higher authority before benefits can be approved—a step that may take another three to five years before benefits are granted.

Example of a Claim Based on Secondary Disabilities

Once you have a copy of your claim file, pertinent laws, and regulations and have identified the evidence to support your claim, you are ready to state your case in writing. The following sample is offered as a guide in organizing your arguments to establish service connection for a secondary medical condition.

This is a claim to establish service connection for a right shoulder disorder secondary to my service-connected left forearm amputation. The Wichita, Kansas, Regional Office granted service connection for a combat injury on February 10, 1969. I was rated 70 percent disabled for a minor left forearm amputation under rating code 5123.

On January 10, 1997, I slipped and fell on the ice in front of my home, which resulted in a right scapulohumeral joint injury. My right arm broke the fall because I instinctively protected the left amputated arm from additional injury. The fall caused a right (major) chronic Grade 2 Rotary Cuff tendinitis condition secondary to instability of the dominant right scapulohumeral joint. The attached medical evidence also provides clinical evidence of moderate to marked instability with three of three positive impingement signs.

Dr. Raymond Scott, my non-VA orthopedic surgeon, notes in his medical evaluation dated March 3, 1997, that the injury has resulted in a greatly reduced range of motion of the right arm. He states that the range of motion is limited to the distance midway between my side and shoulder; movement beyond this point produces severe pain.

Dr. Scott's evaluation points out that based on the

VA evaluation standards in 38 CFR Part 4, the injury to the right shoulder would be considered at least 50 percent disability for the right shoulder. The evaluation specifically points out that this type of disability is consistent with an injury where only one arm was available to break the fall. He further stated that if I had a complete left arm I would not have sustained this type of injury.

I was granted social security disability benefits effective June 1, 1997, based on the left forearm amputation and the limited use of the right arm. Please also consider this an informal application for total disability based on individual unemployability.

In support of my claim, the following evidence is attached and made part of this claim: copies of Dr. Raymond Scott's treatment records between January 12, 1997, and June 1, 1997; Dr. Scott's complete medical assessment dated March 4, 1997; my sworn statement detailing the circumstances of my fall on the ice and my inability to be employed; a letter from my former employer who terminated me because I could no longer perform my duties; and a sworn statement from my wife stating I have tried to find work but have been repeatedly disqualified because I have essentially lost the use of both arms.

Chapter 5 Highlights

Knowing that rating board members are extremely limited in sorting out complex medical issues, the claimant must carefully build his evidence package at a lay level of understanding. Some of the many factors affecting rating boards decisions are inexperience, very little time to assess and study a claim, no medical or legal training to provide a basic level of understanding, and failure to follow regulations and procedures when reviewing a claim.

Rating board members are permitted a great deal of discretion when deciding the merits of a claim. If they don't understand your evidence and how it links to your service-connected condition, they will deny the claim and your only alternative is to file an appeal. If you read the remand decisions of the BVA, you will quickly lose confidence in local VARO rating board members. Case after case is remanded for the most basic reasons. Some of these reasons should have been learned in Rating Board 101: "What I should know before I decide a claim."[2]

VA physicians performing C&P Examinations seldom follow the procedures required of them by the *Physician's Guide for Disability Evaluation Examinations*. All too often, the appointed examiner knows nothing of your problem until you walk through his door.

The examiner often does not have your claim file, or if it was sent from the VARO, did not read it. The examination often fails to follow and report certain mandatory procedures associated with the type of examination requested. More likely than not, the examiner is not a full-time VA medical staff member.

When a flawed examination report is returned to the rating board, the board is supposed to return it for compliance with standard examining procedures. In the thirteen years I hand-wrestled with them, I never had a case where the exam was returned to the hospital on the initiative of the rating board member. Instead, the claims were decided on an examination that was flawed.

---

[2] If you have Internet access, visit http://www.va.gov/Vetapp95. Pick a subject and read the BVA decisions. You may come away wondering if the local ROs know what it means to have a "duty to assist."

The usual sequence of events that followed was an appeal of the decision with an argument that the exam was flawed, and why. The appeal would make its way to the BVA after several years, when it would be remanded to the VARO instructing it to order a *thorough and contemporaneous examination* with a specialist, which was supposed to have been done several years earlier when the claim was first processed. Do not make the mistake of expecting the VA to make your claim for you. Yes, the law does say that if you submit a well-grounded claim, the VA has a duty to assist. But only one person can make your claim: you. You must know what is required before benefits can be granted, then hand the VA all the necessary proof tied up in a neat package.

Make certain you get copies of all medical records associated with your claim. Obtain a copy of your complete claim file so you can provide your doctor with the medical evidence pertaining to your service-connected disability. Now when he prepares your assessment it will be on the basis of evidence and not a hearsay account of what you, his patient, said happened. You will want to provide your doctor with a copy of the section of 38 CFR Part 4 that pertains to the disability being claimed. The report that is prepared on your behalf should state how the doctor rates your disability using VA standards. Make certain that the report states that because of your service-connected disability, the condition being claimed is secondary to that service-connected medical condition.

Remember, you have a duty to submit a well-grounded claim. Unless you do this, your claim is going to be denied and you are going to have an extremely difficult task of trying to salvage it. There is only one way to win: send in a claim that contains evidence that demands the benefits be granted. There are no shortcuts.

C&P Examinations: The Second Weak Link

The Department of Veterans Affairs' Health Administration is actually a multipurpose agency, and the first weak link in the adjudication function at all VAROs. The agency has four primary functions: first, mandatory inpatient and outpatient treatment for service-related disabilities; second, treatment of non-service-related injuries and diseases based on the availability of medical services and patients' financial resources; third, conducting C&P Examinations; and fourth, medical research.

The purpose of this chapter is to make you aware of what the VA must do when it conducts a C&P Examination, how the exam is supposed to be done, and what you must do if the procedures prescribed by the statutes, regulations, and case law are not followed. Most important, you'll learn what to do if you are not given a thorough and contemporaneous medical examination. Millions of veterans are cheated out of lawful benefits because of flawed C&P Examinations and the flawed interpretation of these examinations by rating board members who have neither medical nor legal training or experience.

VA Health Administration

Before we focus on the VA's responsibility to administer C&P Examinations, a general discussion of the overall operation of the VA Health Administration is in order. During the latter part of 1997, VA medical service has come under the scrutiny of both Congress and the public because of abusive management styles; condoning of sexual harassment of patients and employees; many unnecessary deaths of veterans in VA medical facilities; and congressional pressure to cut operating costs and reduce services. During a nineteen-month period (mid-1997 to late 1998), more than three thousand medical mistakes that resulted in more than seven hundred deaths were documented.

Here are some newspaper headlines capturing the public's attention that have weakened the trust and confidence in VA medical care:

"Deaths, federal probe surface at VA centers"
"Disabled VA doctor's assignment criticized, managed care?"
"VA hospital leads nation in settlements"
"VA managers grilled on patient deaths"
"Families ask VA: Did you treat our loved ones properly?"
"VA focus on fatal errors"
"House to review harassment at VA"
"Under fire, VA administrator leaves"
"Deaths haunt Miami VA hospital"
"Troubles at small VA hospital mirror agency overall"
"Lawsuit sparks new investigation of VA doctor"[1]

On November 1, 1997, the *St. Petersburg Times* released a story by David Dahl (*Times* Washington Bureau Chief) that should have sent chills up the spine of anyone seeking medical care from the VA. It is a real horror story about the VA management's decision to assign a physically disabled physi-

[1] *St. Petersburg (Florida) Times,* April 1997 through November 1997.

cian to medical officer of the day (MOD) duties. The inspector general's report stated that patients might have missed a "second chance" because the doctor would have been unable to revive a patient or perform other vigorous procedures. In one particular incident the patient did die. Whether the patient could have survived his medical emergency had the MOD been physically capable will never be known. At this same VA hospital, the director assigned a dentist to be medical chief of staff who in turn supervised all the medical activities of doctors and was responsible for resolving questions of medical policy.

Prescription for Change: A VA Vision

The VA's under secretary for Health, Dr. Kenneth W. Kizer, published a manifesto for change in March 1996, which is expected to have a major impact on veterans healthcare programs in this new century. This seventy-one-page document entitled "Prescription for Change" contains his instructions to the VA Health Administration regarding what he expects and how he wants it accomplished.[2] After a quick reading of his doctrine, one gets the feeling the VA Health Administration will bend over backwards to produce a first-rate healthcare program for all veterans. However, after a closer reading, one realizes that many of the goals and actions could be used to dismantle or reduce the effectiveness of healthcare for veterans. Hundreds of millions of dollars are going to be surgically removed from veterans' healthcare programs. Once all these monies are removed, it is doubtful that they will ever find their way back to the taxpayer.

---

[2] This document can be downloaded from the VA website (http://www.va.gov/health).

To discuss the entire doctrine is not the purpose of this chapter. However, several issues call for awareness because they reflect the overall plan of things to come. Accomplishment of these goals will be easy to achieve because veterans singly or in groups remain impassive and apathetic. Politicians and VA upper management know this and conduct business as usual. The issues are as follows:

- "The Mission of the New VA. The mission of the veteran healthcare system is to serve the needs of America's veterans. It does so by providing specialized care *for the service-connected veterans* [emphasis added], primary care, and related medical and social support services." By its failure to include in its mission statement other groups of veterans currently receiving medical care, the VA has postured itself to wean all others from the system. Again, the only motivation can be one of cutting the cost of veterans services. This is the action of high-level bureaucrats bending to the pressures of Republican and Southern Democrats to do whatever is necessary to cut operating costs of VA health care.
- Change the current hospital-bed-based system to an ambulatory-care-based system. This would include a major shift in surgical care. Every operation that could be performed in a day surgery would be, and the patient would be sent home by the end of the day. According to the VA's own figures, it has already eliminated thirty-five thousand hospital beds within the 170 VAMCs. Currently, fewer than fifty thousand hospital beds are available nationwide. By terminating a hospital bed at a VA hospital, you also eliminate the cost of and need for doctors, physi-

cian's assistants, nurse practitioners, nurse therapists, medical supplies, drugs, related medical specialists, food, cooks, bakers, and kitchen help.

- The doctrine accepts the premise that healthcare support by the federal government will be lessened as the Republican and Southern Democrat politicians push harder to disengage the government from its obligation to support healthcare for its citizens. Therefore, services and care must be cut drastically. Competition will be great for the few available bones that Congress sees fit to toss out.

- The VA accepts that technological innovation will spearhead more care in nonhospital settings, thus further reducing its obligation in hospital and outpatient clinics to care for veterans. By accepting such strategies, the VA implies that it can further reduce operating costs. If this situation occurred in the private sector, the managers would be elated over the black-ink profit reported on the balance sheet.

- The doctrine embraces the proposition that nonphysician caregivers will be increasingly used in healthcare systems of the future. The VA Health Administration is already advancing this concept as it increases the duties of physician's assistants and nurse practitioners in caring for veterans. There is an enormous dollar savings when doctors can be replaced with physician's assistants or nurse practitioners, though at great expense to the veteran.

- The VA tells us that we should keep in mind that while the environment in which VA now operates requires that greater attention be given to the financial management of the system, this should not be misinterpreted as a change in focus or a commercialization of the VA's mission. The

VA Health Administration now accepts patients of retired military members under a combined program offered by the Department of Defense (TRICARE for Life) and Medicare. Both the Department of Defense and Medicare reimburse the VA for medical services rendered.

• The last item is Objective 37 (page 71), in which the VA Health Administration lays out plans to help employees readjust after being terminated by a congressional RIF (Reduction in Forces). "Career transition centers" will be established at each medical center, which means that the upper-level bureaucrats and politicians alike already know what the writing on the wall is saying and what they plan to do about it.

To understand the implications of this last point, suppose a mandated congressional RIF is ordered; using the new group priority system will automatically reduce the number of veterans eligible for medical care. If the VA does not have sufficient staff, how can it continue to treat so many veterans in the lower priority groups?

The Other Side of the Coin: Contradicting VA Hoopla

To create a medical environment influenced primarily by budget considerations that dictate the degree of care available is a wanton disregard of the intent of the laws authorizing medical care of veterans. Every effort of VA healthcare management strives to cut operational costs without any concern for the effect on patients. For example, employing physicians who have to meet only minimum standards to practice medicine has generated great savings. In the private sector, if a doctor moves from New York to Florida, he must be relicensed in

Florida in order to practice medicine. Not so with the VA. Title 38 U.S. Code Chapter 74, Section 7402, requires only that a doctor graduate from a medical school approved by the secretary (which could be anywhere); complete an internship satisfactory to the secretary (no standards prescribed in the law); and be required to obtain only a one-time license to practice medicine, surgery, or osteopathy in any state. Over the years the press has reported cases in which a doctor whose license was revoked by one state's medical board was now practicing medicine for the VA in another state without having to be relicensed.

No other professional standards are demanded of VA doctors. Requiring only minimum professional experience for the VA means lower salaries. The law also allows VA hospitals to hire doctors on a fee basis or a part-time basis, or hire interns and resident student doctors. These would-be doctors comprise nearly 30 percent of all doctors in the VA system.

THE VA PHYSICIAN PROGRAM:
WHAT THE FACTS SAY

The VA Health Administration published three statistical analyses in 1996 which provide considerable insight into the type of treatment administered by VA physicians; the number of full-time or part-time physicians, dentists, and nurses employed nationwide; and how the services of fee-basis physicians are used. The VA healthcare system is divided into twenty-two Veterans Integrated Service Networks (VISNs). Within each VISN regional area, all the VAMCs and outpatient clinics are identified.

Nationwide the VA employs 10,859 physicians, broken down as follows: 7,203 full-time; 2,899 part-time; and 757 resident student. At first, this might look like a well-staffed program for the 170 medical centers. However, many of these medical centers have satellite clinics that must be supported by these hospitals; therefore, the physician support strength in a VAMC is reduced.

According to the VA figures, these 10,859 physicians treated over 28 million patients during 1996 of which 1,639,757 were not veterans. This group of nonveterans treated by the VA included employees, sharing-agreement patients, other federal agencies' patients, and 621,122 patients identified only as "all other." The VA did not publish the doctor-to-patient ratio for 1996, but with nearly one-third of all the doctors being either part-time physicians or resident student doctors, it's easy to see why the VA medical services are up to their eyebrows in quicksand.

The current system of physician-to-patient ratio is not based on the number of patients seen at any given VAMC. Looking at three of the very largest metropolitan areas—Chicago, Illinois; Boston, Massachusetts; and The Bronx, New York—where VAMCs are located, you can see the inequities of the current system. Boston VAMC treated 157,897 outpatients in 1996 while Hines VAMC (Chicago) treated 320,511 outpatients during the same period. Boston's VAMC physician staff included 83 full-time doctors, 72 part-time doctors, and 61 resident student doctors, for a total of 215 physicians, while Hines VAMC (Chicago) was staffed with 82 full-time doctors, 68 part-time doctors, and 72 resident student doctors, for a total of 221 physicians. In The Bronx, New York, VAMC treated 256,151 patients with 83 full-time doctors, 31 part-time doctors, and 9 resident student doctors, for a total of 123 physicians. Under such a system there is no way the VA can insist its care is superior or at the very least comparable to the best in the private sector.

USING PART-TIME AND FEE-BASIS PHYSICIANS

Many VA hospitals hire retired doctors with only a general medical background to conduct C&P Examinations and to perform other medical services that would normally require the skills of a specialist. The Bay Pines, Florida, VAMC used fee-basis doctors to conduct more than twelve thousand C&P Examinations at a unit dollar cost of $88.11 per visit. According to records for 1996, Bay Pines had eight part-time doctors on their rolls. So if these eight doctors conducted 12,140 C&P Examinations and performed some sort of medical service for another 27,246 patients, as records indicate, each doctor averaged treating 4,923 patients in 1996. Considering that these are part-time physicians who work no more than eighty hours per month, each patient received no more than twelve minutes of a doctor's time.

The unfairness of using fee-basis or part-time nonspecialist physicians for a veteran's C&P Examination is best demonstrated by a case I worked on. An 80-year-old retired physician on fee-basis status was employed as a C&P examiner and conducted psychiatric examinations. The VA profited because many veterans with psychiatric disorders were never properly evaluated and thus were denied or given benefits at a rate less than they were entitled to. Also, he was cheap help compared with the cost of full-time board-certified psychiatrists. Because of the flawed examination administered by this doctor, it took years of appeal time before I recaptured my client's 100 percent total disability rating. This long delay was also due to the stubbornness of the local rating boards to acknowledge the exam was flawed. The adjudication division at this VARO was simply not concerned with the rights of this veteran.

The fee-basis program is very much like piecework. The VA doctors conduct so many examinations and for that they receive so much compensation for work performed. This is without a doubt one of the greatest travesties of the alleged concern the VA keeps spewing out about medical treatment for veterans.

HORROR STORIES FROM THE INTERNET AND OTHER SOURCES

Frustrated by the quality of C&P Examinations being offered to veterans, I surveyed veterans throughout the United States via the Internet to see if the poor examination standard my veterans were experiencing was standard nationwide. From the replies I received the answer was a unified *yes*. Examinations were generally substandard throughout the VA healthcare network. Following is the text of my message:

> I am trying to determine if the quality of Compensation & Pension Examinations administered by the Evaluation Unit at VAMC Bay Pines, Florida, is equal to examinations conducted at other VAMCs. In the VAMC Bay Pines catchment area, when a veteran reports for a specialty examination, a specialist will not examine him. The policy of this hospital is to contract primarily retired generalists or other less qualified medical staff on a fee basis and assign them to evaluate complex medical problems. Examples include the following: a resident student studying internal medicine at the University of South Florida Medical School was used to evaluate a mental

disorder caused by a frontal lobe trauma; a female veteran claiming service connection for a total hysterectomy was examined by a nurse; a veteran claiming service connection for cervical and lumbosacral injuries was given a ten-minute examination by a 70-year-old general practitioner. Each of the examples above had one common denominator: the Florida regional office denied them all benefits. Here are some additional facts about examinations conducted at VAMC Bay Pines, Florida: most examinations lasted less than twenty minutes; the examiner did not have the veteran's file at the time of the examination; the results of lab tests and X rays were not reviewed before the C&P examiner completed and signed his report; the examiner made no reference to what extent the disabilities affected the veteran's ability to function under the ordinary conditions of daily life including employment; and the examiner did not follow the evaluation procedures outlined in the *Physician's Guide for Disability Evaluation Examinations* (IB 11-56). In each example cited above, when the veteran was evaluated by his own specialist, the clinical picture was that of a disabled person entitled to compensatory benefits.

I've selected a cross section of typical responses by veterans frustrated with the way they have been treated during C&P Examinations, replies to my inquiries, and accounts of malpractice in VA medical facilities.

Horror Story #1: Failure to Examine All Conditions
"After my exam was completed, I asked the doctor if I had any other comp/pen [C&P] exams. He looked at my file and said, 'No, why do you ask?' I told him I have other disabilities

rated at lesser amounts (0% and 10%) and that I find it discon-
certing that the VA keeps making me take exams for the 100
percent rated disability, but they never check my other disabilities to see if they have changed. The doctor then said, verbatim,
'What good would it do to have them increased? You are getting
100 percent now. Don't you think you've already received more
than your fair share?'

Horror Story #2: Examination without Claim File
"My claim folder was not present during this series of C&P
Exams! I know you stated before when I discussed with you
about them not being present when I had my original exam
that they were required to be present. Does this hold true for
the reevaluation, even though it was not a complete C&P but
only for ratings of 10 percent or more? No formal test was
done as during my original exam in 1994, two years to the
date of the exam I took."

Horror Story #3: Flawed C&P Examination
"How in the hell can these quacks they use for comp and pen
[C&P] get away with that crap? My first comp and pen doc
was 125 years old and the only thing he was interested in was
my coat. He drooled and wrote and wrote an exam that had
nothing to do with issues. It took me five years to get it straight-
ened out. Social Security wanted to send me to him and I told
them I would rather lose the benefits than see him because I
would likely choke him to death if in the same room."

Horror Story #4: Inadequate Examination
"Pete, just so you don't feel too bad about your SSOC [Supple-
mental Statement of the Case] doctor and examination I shall
relate what happened to me. I went in, waited twenty minutes

to be seen. The nurse took about twenty-five minutes to examine me. The doctor walked in and looked at me for about four minutes, had me walk four steps, beat on my knees for a few minutes without eliciting any reaction. Wrote a five-page report that there was nothing wrong with me. No mention of my spinal cord being pressured in two places and that I can't walk straight. Ignored everything I said and that the VA said."

Horror Story #5: Rating Board Ignored C&P Findings
"Even worse is when the Florida VARO denies a claim after THEIR OWN DOCTOR supports it. It happened to me and probably thousands of others. The fact of the matter is VA adjudicators are lawbreakers, and they do it with impunity. Until that fact is addressed and corrected, nothing will change. Sadly, the people who could do something don't have the guts."

Horror Story #6: Disregard for Exam Protocol
"I have clients all over the United States, and I can assure you that the problems you mentioned in your note are common at all VAMCs. It is difficult to quantify any discrepancies. The one thing that you mentioned in your note that is very important is the fact the comp and pen [C&P] doctors did not have a copy of the veteran's claims file from the regional office when they conducted their exam. If that happens the veteran should write to the VA regional office immediately after the exam and complain that the comp and pen doctor did not have his file at the time of the exam. The United States Court of Appeals for Veterans Claims has repeatedly held that such an exam is faulty and cannot be used to rate the veteran. One thing I would do is to have the veteran submit a medical report from his private physician, along with a summary of the physician's qualifications. At the same time, he can submit a written demand

to know the qualifications of the physician who examined him at the VA medical center."

Horror Story #7: Murder

In mid-January 1998 the press reported that a VA physician employed in an Oklahoma VAMC was indicted for the alleged murder of an elderly veteran. The veteran died in 1994 from a willful and deliberate injection of potassium chloride. Information leaking out from behind closed doors suggests that for years the VA hospital administration knew of the event. The VA kept the physician on staff, removing him from direct patient care and assigning him to conduct physical examinations to determine a veteran's eligibility for benefits. The article disclosed that the physician had negotiated a deal with the acting chief of staff to conduct C&P Examinations until he could retire. For this service he was paid $121,000 per year.

Horror Story #8: Substandard Treatment

More than 1,500 miles east of where a murder indictment was issued on a VA physician, two New York VAMCs were cited for poor patient care, filthy conditions, and faulty recordkeeping. The findings of the medical investigation teams concluded that errors in judgment by VA physicians were the root cause of most patient problems. What really is scary is that the hospital administration failed to verify the medical background of many of their doctors. They should have looked for confirmation and success of residency training, the adequacy of training at and standards of foreign medical schools attended by some of the doctors, and whether the doctors were board certified, had been disciplined by the state medical board licensing them to practice, or had had their licenses revoked by a state board.

Veterans' Healthcare Eligibility Reform Act of 1996

In September 1997, the VA Health Administration announced another new healthcare strategy that discreetly further distanced itself from promises made for medical care to veterans who served their country. Veterans seeking medical care after October 1998 were (and still are) required to apply annually for enrollment in the VA healthcare program at which time they are assigned to one of seven priority groups. Failure to apply makes the veteran ineligible to receive medical treatment.[3] Exactly what care you receive is determined by the group to which you are assigned. The career bureaucrats and tax-cutting politicians were looking for a way of limiting medical support for a very large aging veteran population. Bureaucrats will never earn the brownie points necessary to enjoy the favor of a Republican politician unless they can cut the cost of operating the VA so the money can be spent on Republican projects.

It's not a big stretch to relate this program to the story of Robin Hood. Only, in this version, "Robin VA" takes from those in need of help and returns millions of dollars to the king's coffers so the monies can be used for more important projects that do not deal with the needs of people.

There is another feature of this new healthcare program veterans should know about. The veteran's eligibility status is evaluated annually by the primary care center to determine if

---

[3] Exceptions: if you are rated by the VA as having a service-connected disability of 50 percent or more; were discharged or separated from the service with a compensable disability and it has been less than a year since your separation; or you are seeking care from the VA for only a service-connected disability.

they will remain in their current priority group, be assigned to a lower priority group, or be terminated from the program. For example, let's assume you were assigned to Priority Group 2 when first enrolled because you have a 30 percent service-connected disability. However, the VA rating board reduced your current rating to 0 percent based on their interpretation of the results of a recent C&P Examination. You have now been identified as Group 6 eligible, which translates to continued priority care for your service-related condition only. For unrelated, non-service-connected medical problems you are dropped to almost the lowest level of care. Don't despair, for there is a bright side to this demotion: if you do get care for a non-service-related medical problem, the VA will not charge you a copayment fee for the treatment.

Veterans Millennium Healthcare and Benefits Act 1999

On November 30, 1999, the Veterans Millennium Healthcare and Benefits Act (PL 106-117) was signed into law. The act addressed long-term care healthcare issues along with day-to-day adult healthcare needs. This new statute adds subsection 1710A and 1710B to Title 38 U.S. Code, Part II, Chapter 17 to spell out who is eligible for long-term nursing home care. Briefly, eligibility is extended to any veteran who requires nursing home care for a service-related injury or disease and to any veteran who needs such care for any reason if he has a service-connected disability rated 70 percent or more. This new entitlement dealing with granting benefits for any condition may be very narrow in scope depending how the term "disability rated 70 percent" is interpreted. There are two ways a veteran could be rated 70 percent disabled by the VA: a single disability could be rated 70 percent or multiple disabilities could collectively qualify as a 70 percent rating.

Compensation and Pension Examination

Almost all service-connected benefits extended to veterans rely on some degree of disability that was incurred in the service, aggravated in the service, or resulted from treatment in a VA facility by VA medical staff. Veterans wishing to apply for non-service-connected pension benefits must also prove they are sufficiently disabled to be rendered unemployable. The claim process for service connection requires the VA to obtain original service medical records, medical records from VA treatment centers (hospitals or clinics), copies of records from private physicians, and hospital records before deciding the merits of the claim.

38 CFR §3.326(a) states that where a reasonable probability of a valid claim is indicated, a Department of Veterans Affairs examination will be authorized. However, the regulation also permits the rating board to decide the claim based on the findings of a private physician if the report meets certain standards. The specialist's report must include clinical manifestations and substantiation of diagnosis by findings of diagnostic techniques generally accepted by the medical authorities. Pathological studies, X rays, and laboratory tests must be part of the specialist's assessment.

If the records are not sufficient to determine the current degree of disability, or if the rating board elects not to accept the specialist's report for any reason, a C&P Examination will be scheduled. Herein lies a major unfairness to veterans. The medical expertise of the examining physician is left to the discretion of the medical service. In my thirteen years working with veterans as an advocate, I don't recall a single case where a board-certified doctor specializing in the condition being evaluated examined the veteran. All C&P Examinations were administered by non-VA staff doctors who were recruited from the ranks of retired doctors. Many of the doctors I inquired about through the AMA headquarters in Chicago were identified as family practice physicians or general practitioners. A while back, using Prodigy's Veteran's Bulletin Board, I asked if it was a common practice throughout the United States for veterans to be examined by these fee-basis general practitioners. The responses were not surprising: C&P Examinations by nonspecialist doctors is a common practice of VAMCs.

The only time a general practitioner cannot be used is when an appeal is remanded to the VARO and the remand order instructs that the claimant be examined by a board-certified specialist. VA manual M 21-1 Part VI, Change 38, dated August 30, 1995, mandates this procedure be followed. Yet the VA assigns whoever it pleases, not necessarily a board-certified doctor. In many cases it is the same doctor who did the initial evaluation. And I've yet to see a document in a claimant file showing that the rating board refused to accept the examination, mandating the medical center assign a board-certified specialist.

This is why it's important for you to know the medical specialty of the examining physician; it's the basis for an appeal if benefits are denied. The court has held many times that the VA has a duty to provide you with a thorough and contemporaneous examination. When you have a complex medical problem and a retired general practitioner examines you, a red flag should go up.

C&P EXAMINATIONS

The process starts when a claim is filed for any benefit involving a disability or disease that was incurred in the service. Your claim and medical evidence are forwarded to the adjudication division where the medical evidence attached to your claim and service medical records are reviewed. By law, the rating board can rate your claim just on this evidence if it deems it adequate for rating purposes.

The first hurdle is that the claim must be recognized as well-grounded. If the evidence does not suggest that the claim is plausible, meritorious on its own, or capable of substantiation, the claim will be denied. If this decision is rendered, the veteran will spend the next three to five years arguing only one point: did the submitted evidence support a well-grounded claim?

Assuming the claim meets the standards of being well grounded, the law mandates that the VA has a duty to assist the veteran from this point forward. When the rating board cannot make a rating based on the medical evidence submitted with the claim and the service medical records, it must request a C&P Examination from a VA medical facility. The veteran should be scheduled for a thorough and contemporaneous examination—more commonly referred to as a C&P Examination—by the medical facility closest to his home.

It is the rating board that tells the medical facility what kind of examination to conduct. The request is forwarded electronically through the Automated Medical Information Exchange (AMIE). In most cases the rating board orders only a general evaluation with no request for a specialist.

Even if the rating board requested a specialty examination, the hospital is not obligated to assign a specialist. They have complete freedom to assign whomever they choose. Through the years I have seen them assign only fee-basis doctors or resident student doctors from a local medical school to evaluate complex medical problems claimed by the veteran. Downsizing of hospital staffing and tightly controlled fiscal budget restraints make the practice of contracting fee-basis physicians an ideal choice. As for veterans receiving an examination that is actually thorough and contemporaneous, the best that can be said for the practice is that it is a farce.

Never forget this: the VA Benefits Administration and VA Health Administration are like two families who have the same last name but are unrelated. Each function is not accountable to the other for its actions and no real central authority exists to control these two agencies.

However, 38 CFR §4.2, "Interpretation of an Examination Report," requires the rating specialist to return the examination report when the diagnosis is not supported by the findings or if the examination report does not contain sufficient details. Rating boards seldom if ever return C&P Examinations unless the veteran or the advocate has protested that the examination was inadequate and thus flawed. Rating boards can easily deny benefits when the exam protocol fails to follow the examining procedures outline in VA Medical Manual IB 11-56 *Physician's Guide for Disability Evaluation Examinations.* I've never seen a rating board member study the results of a C&P Examination to ensure that the report submitted was in full compliance with VA Manual IB 11-56. There are several reasons for this, one of which is that the shallow level of understanding of rating board members' knowledge of medicine is not sufficient for them to detect the flawed nature of the examination. All you have to do is look at the remand and reversal rate of appeals reviewed by the BVA (between 70% and 80% nationwide) to know that rating boards are extremely deficient in the interpretation and application of the concepts related to law and medicine.

AMIE C&P Examination Program

AMIE is a multipurpose electronic system used to exchange information between medical centers, outpatient clinics, and regional offices. One program within AMIE is the AMIE C&P Examination Program. The program allows VAROs to electronically transmit examination requests to medical centers. After the medical center prints the requests and schedules specific examinations, standardized examination worksheets are printed. The printed request and worksheet now become the official record between the VARO and medical center.

It is important for veterans to know exactly what the examination process is all about. When your claim is denied, a major part of your appeal will involve proving that the VA did not follow regulations, manuals, statutes, and case law. Obtaining copies of the records generated during the examination process is absolutely essential should you have to go head-to-head with the VA in a dispute challenging its decision. Briefly, the program is as follows:

- The VARO office clerk electronically inputs the request to the VAMC.
- Upon receipt of the request the medical center clerk schedules the exam.
- Worksheets are printed and the examination is scheduled.
- Using printed worksheets, the examiner conducts the examination.
- The examiner dictates the report using the worksheet format.
- The transcriber enters the results into the systems and

routes a printed copy to the physician for review and signature.

- The examination report is electronically dispatched to the VARO.
- The report is printed by the VARO clerk and forwarded to the rating board for action.

A copy of the following records should be requested from the VARO: initial request for C&P Examination transmitted to the medical facility; the doctor's report furnished to the VARO; and any lab reports, X rays, and special tests performed and sent to the VARO. From the VA medical facility performing the C&P Examination, you'll need copies of the following: the worksheet used by the examining physician, the dictated report of the examination, test results, radiological reports, lab results, and a statement from the medical facility of the physician's qualifications.

PROCEDURES FOR C&P EVALUATION EXAMINATIONS

The *Physician's Guide for Disability Evaluation Examinations* (IB II-56) provides the VA examiner with very specific instructions as to how an examination should be conducted when evaluating a veteran. All physicians and dentists are issued this manual to provide current guidance in examining claimants for disabilities being claimed. The policies set forth in this manual apply to all VA physicians, staff doctors, fee-basis physicians, part-time doctors, and resident student doctors training at a VAMC.

There are four important reasons why it is absolutely necessary to obtain a copy of the pertinent chapters of this manual before you are examined: first, you want to know if the examining VA physician is in fact following the procedures set forth to ensure every aspect of your condition is evaluated; second, when you read the report forwarded to the rating board member by the examining physician, you must be able to determine if the physician did in fact conduct all the required tests and evaluation procedures associated with your particular medical condition; third, the report as filed must include very specific medical findings and opinions by the examining physician; and fourth, if you arrange for a private specialist to evaluate your condition or review the results of the VA examination, he will have to know what is supposed to be reported in terms of medical findings or interpretation of test results. The reason I stress these four reasons can best be illustrated by this analogy: if you were injured in an automobile accident and sustained a lifetime disability, would you take the word of an insurance company doctor as to how disabling your injuries were? The only interest of any insurance company is to see how cheaply it can settle the claim. The degree of your lifetime limitations, pain, or loss of income does not enter into the equation.

Physician's Guide **Highlights**
In most cases the C&P Examination is not conducted by a board-certified specialist. Hospital administration is given full discretion as to who will be assigned duties of evaluating veterans for the purpose of determining entitlement to benefits. Authorization from the **central office** in Washington, D.C., has quietly granted the use of physician's assistants, nurse practitioners, residents from one of the local teaching hospitals, and retired general practitioners hired on a part-time basis to conduct C&P Examinations. The *Physician's Guide for Disability Evaluation Examinations* (hereinafter called the *Physician's Guide*) does not reference the use of this type of medical

staff, who are at the bottom of the totem pole of medical specialists. The manual refers to physicians only.

When a veteran is evaluated for a service-connected disability, the regulations and manuals specifically require the use of a physician to perform the evaluation. When you are scheduled for a C&P Examination, do not assume that because the examination is being conducted in a VAMC the examiner is a trained specialist in the area being evaluated. The veteran must ask the doctor what his qualifications are and if he is board certified. If not, immediately following the examination notify the VARO *in writing* that you did not receive a thorough and contemporaneous examination because the hospital failed to provide a specialist for the condition being evaluated. When putting the VA on notice that your evaluation was not in compliance with published directives, make certain you mail your complaint to the VA by certified mail with return receipt. Failure to do so could cost you thousands of dollars down the road.

The *Physician's Guide* is a general introduction to what is expected of VA examiners. It is an outline of VA hospital administration policy, which every examining physician is required to follow. Every physician who examines claimants should be familiar with the material contained in this guide and in the VA rating schedule. Failure to follow the policies and procedures set forth is grounds to appeal a denial of benefits or a rating that is below the true level of severity experienced by the claimant.

Schedule for Rating Disabilities
Part 4 of 38 CFR is the official guide for converting clinical findings to standardized diagnostic codes and grades of severity. The purpose of furnishing the VA Schedule for Rating Disabilities (38 CFR Part 4) to VAMCs and clinics is to familiarize

physicians performing disability examinations with the principle and practices of rating boards in the application of the rating schedule. The *Physician's Guide* presents explanations and techniques for performing examinations that will meet the specific requirements of the rating schedule. Joint conferences between examining physicians and adjudication personnel staff are declared necessary to provide the highest quality of medical services relating to disability evaluations.

Importance and Purpose of Reports
Physicians are told that the purpose of these examinations is to establish the presence or absence of disease, injuries, or residual conditions and to record findings indicative of the severity of the disabling conditions so that they may be evaluated. An inaccurate examination, or an incomplete or biased one, may deprive a veteran and his family of benefits to which they are entitled. Examinations that are not in compliance with policies and procedures become appealable if benefits are denied.

COMPLETENESS OF REPORTS

The examining physician is responsible for making a complete and detailed report, including correct diagnosis of the disabling condition and a description of the effects of the disability on the veteran's ordinary activity. The correct diagnosis is of great importance. The reports should include the clinical and laboratory findings as well as all other evidence that will substantiate the diagnosis and severity of the disability.

The exact findings recorded are just as important as the actual diagnosis itself in meeting the needs of a rating board member. Similarly, the findings and clinical evidence demonstrating the severity of the disability should be reported, because in most claim actions for compensation benefits, the rating board member never sees the veteran. Clarity of description, legibility of notes, accuracy of dates, identification of normal ranges for tests reported, and other details are very important.

You need to obtain a copy of the C&P Examination and carefully review it to make certain the C&P examiner did in fact convey this detailed information in the report. If this type of information is missing, the rating board member is required under 38 CFR §4.2 to return the examination report as inadequate for evaluation purposes. However, I assure you that rating board members do not routinely return evaluations unless the claimant starts hollering that benefits were denied because the report was inadequate. Failure to check for missing information is one reason why so many claims are denied. The claimant has absolutely no idea what was reported, the significance of the information reported, or the conclusions of examining physician.

SCOPE OF THE EXAMINATION

A request for a C&P evaluation from a rating board member lists all service-connected disabilities—active, static, or alleged. It has been the practice of rating boards to ask for a general medical examination only instead of a specific examination that is directly related to the conditions being claimed. The manual states the scope of the examination should be broad enough to cover all diseases, injuries, and residuals that are alleged by the veteran. Examinations should be made by a specialist where indicated by the disabilities claimed. In *Irby v. Brown, 6 Vet. App. 12 (1994)*, the court held that the VA failed in its duty to assist by not ordering a thorough and contemporaneous psychiatric examination (specialty examination) and as such the report did not give a specific finding.

The way the system works, if you have a serious back disorder with radiating pain, a general practitioner instead of an orthopedist or neurologist will most likely evaluate you. It is totally feasible for the VA to operate by this system because it keeps the cost of care down. However, it is a breach in the doctrine decreed by this country to care for veterans who became disabled while serving the interest of the country.

If the claim was denied based on a C&P Examination administered by a fee-basis general practitioner, file a Notice of Disagreement citing that the VA failed in its duty to assist by not providing a thorough and contemporaneous examination. In addition, cite either *Sklar v. Brown, 5 Vet. App. 140 (1993)*[4] or *Irby v. Brown*, whichever is more applicable. Make certain that you state very clearly the reasons why the C&P Examination was flawed and why the case law is applicable.

GENERAL MEDICAL AND SURGICAL EXAMINATIONS

When the examiner finds specific abnormalities, all necessary studies should be made to arrive at a correct and complete diagnosis, including, if indicated, general medical and surgical examinations. Following the initial general postdischarge physical examination, when only one system is requested, only that

---

[4] In *Sklar v. Brown* the court held that if there is a diagnosis by a specialist and the only evidence against the veteran claim is a contrary opinion by a nonspecialist, then the findings of the nonspecialist should carry little weight.

system will be examined unless a reason for further study becomes apparent during the visit.

When you obtain a copy of your claim file, look for a copy of the order to the medical center requesting that an examination be scheduled. If the rating board member asked for nothing more than a general physical examination and you are claiming a cardiac disorder, for example, challenge any decision denying benefits based on the fact that because you were evaluated by a noncardiac specialist, you were not afforded a thorough and contemporaneous examination.

The C&P evaluation unit considers a general examination to include information about the patient's age, height, weight, personal appearance, nutrition, muscular development, posture, gait, right- or lefthandedness, pulse rate, respiratory rate, temperature, and blood pressure. The *Physician's Guide* also directs that an exercise test should be conducted on all conditions that are manifested by general weakness, easy fatigability, or shortness of breath (dyspnea), unless such a test is inadvisable. If an exercise test cannot be performed, the reasons should be reported.

Of the hundreds of C&P Examinations I have reviewed over the years, most did not focus on the primary medical problem or detail what tests were administered that supported the diagnosis for which the examination was scheduled. The findings reported by these C&P examining physicians were loaded with basic background facts such as age, height, and weight. The doctor's narrative provided very little insight as to what was found, the degree of the disability caused by the condition, or how the disability affected the veteran's ability to work. The evaluation did not indicate what tests were administered or what medical facts led to the diagnosis. I do not ever remember reading a report in which the claimant was given an exercise test because he was exhibiting symptoms of weakness, fatigability, or shortness of breath upon exertion.

SEVERITY OF DISABILITY

When reporting the finding of a C&P evaluation, The *Physician's Guide* emphasizes that "the essential duty of the examining physician is to record a full, clear report of the medical and industrial HISTORY, THE SYMPTOMATOLOGY and PHYSICAL FINDINGS." The purpose is to permit a rating board member to compare the medical findings reported by the examining physician with the disability percentage evaluations contained in the rating schedule. For a client who intended to obtain a medical assessment from a private specialist of his choice, I always made a copy of the rating schedule for the private doctor. This provided the framework for the report to be compared against the VA rating schedule. Thus if the examination report determined the veteran was 60 percent disabled based on solid medical evidence, and the VA rated the claim at 40 percent disabling based only on its own unsubstantiated conclusions, the veteran had a winnable appeal.

REVIEW OF CLAIM FOLDER

The law requires that the veteran's claim file be available to the C&P examiner and must be reviewed by the examiner before the examination. This important policy is violated and ignored by C&P physicians and rating board members alike. The United States Court of Appeals for Veterans Claims and BVA have remanded case after case to local VAROs because they refuse to follow this policy, thus violating the veteran's rights to a fair decision.

The *Physician's Guide* states in part: "Much of the material in the claims folder is of no use to the examining physician. However, some material *is of utmost importance* [emphasis added] in orienting the physician. Particularly important are medical, social, and industrial historical data; physical and laboratory findings of previous examinations (including those made while in active military service); and rating forms showing previous diagnosis and disability ratings. These data must be considered chronologically in order to obtain a true picture of the progress of the disorder. In some cases, the examining physician will find incomplete examinations, unsupported diagnoses, and misuse of terminology. It will be necessary for the examining physician to integrate the situation with the information available by constructing an overall picture that matches the facts available."

If the claim file is not present when you are examined, or if the examining physician has not read the file before the examination, grounds exist to appeal the denial of any benefit sought based on the VA failure to provide you with a thorough and contemporaneous examination. If you do not see your claim file when being examined, ask the attending physician if he has it. If you see the file, ask the doctor, "Have you read the claim file in its entirety?" In either situation, if the answer is no, advise the local VARO immediately in writing that you did not receive a fair and contemporaneous examination because the examiner did not have your file present or was not aware of your case medical history. Make a copy of your letter before sending it by certified mail with return receipt requested.

Preparing for the Examination

The best way to maintain control throughout the entire claims process is to take the initiative. Do not file a claim until you have built a winnable case.

The first step in building a winning case is to file an informal claim. By doing so, the entitlement date is protected and you have up to one year to prepare your claim and obtain all evidence necessary to prove entitlement. For example, let's say that you sustained a back injury in the service that has now been diagnosed as intervertebral disc syndrome. Your condition is characterized as severe recurring attacks with persistent symptoms compatible with sciatic neuropathy. You can no longer be gainfully employed. Physical activity is limited because of the severe chronic pain.

The second step is obtaining copies of all VA regulations, manuals, and pertinent case law that may pertain to your circumstances. Copies of VA regulations (38 CFRs) can be found in your local county law library or on the VA home page on the Internet. Copies of United States Court of Appeals for Veterans Claims decisions can be found at the law library (look for West Publishing Company's *Veterans Appeals Reporter*). The *Physician's Guide for Disability Evaluation Examinations* can be found at all VAMCs, state service officer locations, and county veterans service offices. You will need to copy chapter 1 and the chapter that is pertinent to your condition.

The third step is to arrange an appointment with your personal medical specialist requesting an assessment of your condition. He should have a copy of the 38 CFR Part 4 regulation, chapters from the *Physician's Guide*, copies of any service medical records, and a copy of any lay statements from people knowledgeable about the injury or disease. If others have treated you for these same conditions, obtain copies of these records.

If you do not have a specialist to work with, the local AMA chapter or hospital referral service will provide the names of doctors whose specialty covers your condition. To save yourself grief and unnecessary expense, first determine if the doctor will give you a written assessment of the findings. Without a written report, an evaluation is useless for VA purposes.

The fourth step is to develop a lay statement to support the authenticity of your claim. Unless you file a claim within the first year following your separation, the VA has a nasty habit of denying benefits based solely on the fact that service medical records are silent as to your condition. If the event that caused the injury to your back was not documented in your service records, you can bet the decision will be "claim denied." All lay statements should be in the form of a sworn deposition so that these statements become evidence.

Remember, a statement from family or service friends will not be accepted as valid evidence if the statement is giving a medical opinion. A lay statement can give sworn testimony as to what was witnessed or the limitations observed subsequent to the injury. It is important that before filing the claim, veterans give a sworn detailed statement as to what occurred, where they were treated, and how often they were treated. If the injury occurred during combat with the enemy, then your statement alone is sufficient to establish service incurrence.

The fifth step is to prepare all the supporting evidence to be appended to your claim.

After taking these steps, you will be ready to file your official claim and to take any scheduled C&P Examinations within the following few months.

Taking the Examination

Once you are scheduled for a C&P Examination, you must comply with the order and report to the medical center or clinic or risk being denied benefits.[5] Failure to report can complicate and bias your claim. However, if the condition you are being evaluated for is cyclical—having inactive and active stages— you must contact the medical center and advise them of this fact so you can be rescheduled and evaluated when the condition is active and can be observed by a physician. Failure of the VA to evaluate your condition during an active stage is grounds for a reversal if the claim is denied.[6]

Medical examiners assigned to the C&P Unit are notorious for spending only five to twenty minutes with a patient. The evaluation may be flawed because the examination was all or in most part performed by a physician's assistant, nurse practitioner, or resident student doctor. However, precautions can be taken to reduce the ineffectiveness of an examination by an examiner with limited medical skills:

- Take someone with you if at all possible. This person can attest in a sworn statement that you were in the examining room only "x" number of minutes. Your companion can also testify if you were sent to other medical services at the clinic, and if so, which ones. Try to get your witness into the examining room with you so he can attest to whether your claim file was in fact available at the time of

---

[5] See *Dusek v. Derwinski, 2 Vet. App. 519 (1992)*. In this case it was ruled that the VA properly denied the veteran increased benefits because he failed to report for an evaluation examination and failed to provide a good cause for his action. The court noted, "[t]he duty to assist is not always a one-way street."

[6] See *Ardison v. Brown, 6 Vet. App. 405 (1994)*. The Court ruled the VA failed in its duty to assist by relaying on an examination that was performed during an inactive stage.

the evaluation and whether the doctor was knowledgeable about your medical history.

- Determine the examiner's credentials. Is he a cardiologist, orthopedist, or neurologist, for example? Find out if the doctor is board certified in a specialty and whether he is currently licensed in the state where the examination was conducted. After the examination, write the AMA at its national headquarters in Chicago and obtain a background report on the doctor or doctors who examined you. All this information is necessary if you have to refute the examiner's ability to administer a thorough and contemporaneous examination.

- List your medical problems and describe all the symptoms you are experiencing for each medical condition. If you are on medication, list the drug and dosage of each drug used to treat your problems. If the medication has resulted in side effects that are responsible for other medical problems, record this information and make it known to the examiner.

- Give the examiner a copy of the credentials of and medical assessment by your own private specialist. In many cases this will intimidate or influence an examiner of a lesser medical background. When the VA uses minimally qualified examiners to medically evaluate complex injuries or diseases, a veteran will be able to counter this breach of faith.

Don't Make Assumptions: The VA Is Not Always Right

If your claim is denied, you should not accept the results of a VA medical evaluation as conclusive and absolute. A lot is riding on the results of a C&P Examination, and to assume that the VA administered a thorough and contemporaneous examination is a grave mistake that could deprive you of lawful entitlements and care. Do not assume that the VA examining doctor is an expert in the field related to your disability problems. The services of a recognized private specialist should be obtained to refute the medical findings of any VA physician if benefits are denied. This is the only way to protect your interests.

Chapter 6 Highlights

The entire VA system is undergoing a transformation that is not necessarily in the best interest of veterans. The VA Health Administration is currently engaged in two very ambitious programs that will downsize the VA healthcare system and drastically cut costs.

Under Secretary for Health Dr. Kizer claims his program "Prescription for Change," subtitled "The New VA" will work wonders. The goal is to reduce hospital beds to fewer than fifty thousand nationwide, adopt an ambulatory care system, thus minimizing inpatient care for the 26 million veterans; include treatment for nonveterans such as Medicare patients and Medicaid patients based on contract agreement with other government agencies; and employ more nonphysician caregivers, further reducing the level of skilled care for the very ill veterans. His doctrine tells us that these major changes are about to surface. Every VAMC is preparing to reduce the number of employees across the board. This is the reason they are opening what is known as "Employee Transition Offices." This is where they send the about-to-be-fired employee to suggest other employment opportunities.

The second initiative designed to extract healthcare programs from veterans across the board was made part of the Veterans' Healthcare Eligibility Reform Act of 1996. Veterans desiring medical treatment from the VA had to enroll in the VA healthcare program by October 1998. At the time of enrollment, a veteran was assigned to one of seven priority groups. This program requires every veteran who is not rated at least 50 percent disabled to register annually. The priority group to which a veteran is assigned is not permanent and can be adjusted up or down the priority ladder.

When both programs are implemented and fused into a single purpose, the VA has the structure to limit healthcare to those with service-related conditions. With the exception of veterans rated 50 percent or more, the only treatment available to a veteran who is rated less than 50 percent will be for the actual condition that is service related. Once this goal is achieved, billions of dollars can be redirected to more satisfying political goals totally unrelated to the needs of the citizenry.

Primarily minimally trained examiners perform VA medical examinations. Doing so is cheaper than providing the kind of specialist required to properly evaluate a serious injury or complex disease. The VA is also resorting to using nurse practitioners and physician's assistants to conduct C&P Examinations. Even though they allegedly work under the supervision of a physician, an examination by one of these nonphysician caregivers can be worthless.

It is an absolute necessity for a veteran to consult with a private medical specialist before being examined by the VA. You must provide your specialist with medical records of your condition, VA regulations, and manuals that are applicable to your situation. Your specialist's assessment of your condition must show a clear diagnosis, the limitations it imposes upon you, and how it relates to your contention that it is service incurred. The doctor's closing remarks should contain a statement similar to this:

Based on a review of Mr. Smith's service medical records, my examinations, and tests, it is my opinion that this condition did in fact occur while he served in the U.S. Army between 1945 and 1955. Using the standards published in 38 CFR Part 4, Mr. Smith is 60 percent disabled.

By law, the VA must provide you with a thorough and contemporaneous examination if the medical evidence submitted with your claim and service medical records are not sufficient to rate your claim. You cannot afford to sit back and expect the VA to adjudicate your claim like King Solomon. To be successful you must know exactly what the VA must do when you are examined. Remember that 38 CFR Part 4 and the *Physician's Guide for Disability Evaluation Examinations* are the tools the VA examiner must work with when he evaluates your condition. Know what should be checked, and if he doesn't follow the manual ask why he is not following the procedures mandated in the *Physician's Guide*.

Make certain when you are examined that you ask the examiner for his credentials and whether he read and reviewed your claim file before this examination. Don't let him ignore the question—get an answer. Failure to review your file is a violation not only of the *Physician's Guide* but also of federal law. Make this fact known to him even if he gets huffy because of your question. You cannot afford to be passive in these matters. As soon as the examination has been concluded, go to the waiting room and record everything that was discussed and checked. Record the total time you were with the examiner. If you don't make certain that they dot every i and cross every t, it may cost you three to five years. Rating boards look forward to getting worthless examinations.

7 | PROVE IT OR LOSE IT

Why You Must Support Your Claim with Facts

Properly supporting a well-grounded claim requires facts that cannot be rebutted or dismissed as pure speculation by a rating board member. Failure to substantiate your case will result in an almost immediate denial of the claim. Nothing would suit the VA more than to have a claim based on an unsubstantiated premise that an injury or disease was incurred on active duty. The claim would be denied as not being well grounded.

For the next three to five years, if you persevere, your claim will slowly wiggle its way through the appeal process. The only issue under consideration would be whether the initial claim would lead a reasonable person to believe that it was *possible* that the condition could be service related. Always remember that you have the burden to show a reasonable possibility that your injury or disease occurred on active duty. Until you establish that the claim is well grounded, the VA does not have to lift a finger to help you. And it won't. Don't make the mistake of thinking the VA will take a veteran aside and say, "If you want to get this claim approved, you must prove these points by providing the following types of evidence."

You must stop a moment and ask: "What does the VA require before it will grant benefits for this condition?" "What must I prove?" "What kind of proof do I need?" and "Where do I find this proof?" Then you must assemble a case based on facts that will allow the rating board only one option: to grant the benefit claimed. The goal is to have benefits granted without being forced into a three- to five-year appeal contest. If your claim has to be appealed, make certain the BVA or the Court of Appeals for Veterans Claims will reverse the VARO. You will never win a claim if it's based solely on your own unsubstantiated opinion that your disability is service related.

Knowing What the VA Wants and Where to Look for It

The first step in winning your claim is to determine exactly what the VA requires in order to grant benefits. You must find the references in 38 CFR Parts 3 and 4 that pertain to your claim. You need a copy of all pertinent CFR paragraphs and rating schedules relating to your medical problem. These regulations, statutes, and manuals will tell you exactly what must be established before benefits can be granted. This is an easy but absolutely necessary step in the process of building your case.

Where to Start Looking for Information

Libraries are a rich source of information for a veteran seeking supportive references necessary to the preparation of a claim. Many specialty libraries are available to veterans searching for facts: law libraries, public libraries, Library of Congress, major university libraries, city libraries such as New York Public Library, or medical school libraries such as Harvard University Library. And don't forget the Internet. A veteran can collect a lot of information if he is determined to dig for facts.

LAW LIBRARIES

Every county law library nationwide subscribes to the complete annual printing of the Code of Federal Regulations. The volumes are numbered sequentially and the regulations pertaining to the Department of Veterans Affairs are found in volume 38. Law school libraries also have current copies of these publications.

Four other publications found in law libraries should be researched and supportive information copied. The first is Title 38 U.S. Code and the second is United States Code Annotated (U.S.C.A.) volume 38. The third is the *Federal Register*, the daily publication of changes of government policy and procedures. The fourth is the decisions of the United States Circuit Courts, Federal Courts of Appeals, and United States Court of Appeals for Veterans Claims published in documents called *Reporters*. They include the published decisions for the various federal courts. West Publishing Company is one of the publishers of the federal court system's decisions.

For specific decisions concerning veterans issues, consult West's *Veterans Appeals Reporter*. Here you will find all the final decisions of the United States Court of Appeals for Veterans Claims that have become case law and binding upon the VA and veterans. If the VA or the veteran appealed the court's decision to a higher court, then you must follow the trail all the way through the judicial system to the United States Appeals Court or to the Supreme Court.

Title 38 U.S. Code is the actual statute that governs the operation of the Department of Veterans Affairs. The annotated version, privately published by the West Publishing Company, is extremely valuable because it simplifies the legalese of the statute. This publication is vital to the researcher as it offers many special services such as cross-referencing to CFRs and the legislative history of that section of the statute. Also available are references to certain court cases that may have been a factor in clarifying the meaning of a particular sector of the statute.

Law libraries also maintain a daily release of information published in the *Federal Register*. This is a very important source of information as it contains current changes the VA put into effect or changes they are proposing to implement in the near future.

UNIVERSITY LIBRARIES

Many university libraries throughout the United States have been designated as depositories for government publications and documents. As a citizen you are entitled access to this information on deposit by the government without being a member of the faculty or student body. Available will be all current CFRs and U.S. Statutes (Title 38, for example). You will be able to find changes to VA policy and procedures published in the *Federal Register*. You will not be charged for accessing this information. However, there is usually a nominal charge to copy the documents.

PUBLIC LIBRARIES

Many public libraries maintain a complete set of federal regulations and statutes. The extent and availability of the information will depend on the size of the community supported by the local library system. However, many library systems are now linked in a network. Although the particular library may not have 38 CFR or Title 38 U.S. Code in-house, it may be able to request it from a library within its network.

VA REGIONAL OFFICES

Every VARO has a reference library reading room that is available to the public for research. In addition to having current copies of Title 38 U.S. Code and 38 CFR Parts 3 and 4, they are a rich source of other valuable information that could support your claim. On file will be the VA Manual M-21; VA circulars released by the central office in Washington, D.C.; specific public announcements of policy changes and procedures printed in the *Federal Register*; a complete set of opinions released by the General Counsel; the *Physician's Guide for Disability Evaluation Examinations* (IB 11 56); and decisions rendered by the Court of Veterans Appeals printed in *Veterans Appeals Reporter* by West Publishing Company.

In the event the local regional office will not provide a means for you to copy the information you need, there are other options. First, make an accurate list of each document you want a copy of, making certain to identify the pages, paragraphs, subject titles, and the document name and number. Then go to your congressperson's office and request assistance in obtaining copies of the information you require. This is public information available under the provisions of the Freedom of Information Act. In preparing this book I had to use my congressman's office several times because I was being stonewalled. Do not be timid about using the services of an elected official, as this is one of the important functions they perform.

VA MEDICAL CENTERS AND CLINICS

If you live within a reasonable distance of a VA medical center or clinic, you can obtain a copy of pertinent chapters of the *Physician's Guide* that spell out in detail exactly what the C&P examiner must check and report on.

If you have a patient file at either a VA hospital or clinic, ask for a copy of the entire file. It will support your statement that you are currently being medically treated for this problem. Remember, when the application is filed you must be currently suffering from the residual effects of the injury or disease to have a valid claim. Veterans often came into my office wanting to file a claim for, say, a bad back. They would describe an incident that happened which could account for an injury to the back. However, when I asked the $64,000 question—"What does your doctor say about your condition now and what kind of treatment is being administered?"—I would get an answer such as "Well, I'm not being treated now for it, I just want to get it on the record now so if it starts hurting again I will already be service connected for it." If you file a claim while the condition is not actively causing medical problems, you will lose. You cannot prove entitlement.

More important, you will handicap yourself in the future. The VA will have denied your claim as not being well grounded and treat the active duty medical condition as an acute and transitory incident. To reopen your claim the only option available is to introduce medical evidence that is new and material. This is evidence that was never previously considered and would justify a belief that the current medical problem is directly linked to the back injury on active duty. The more years between the original incident and the current flare-up, the steeper the climb up the face of the mountain.

VETERANS SERVICE OFFICES:
STATE AND COUNTY

The availability of these publications at your local county veterans service office depends upon several factors, one of which is the support the office receives from county commissioners. If the commissioners understand the importance of this service to the community, and if the budget is sufficient to properly run an advocacy program, the office will most likely have the publications discussed.

The second factor is whether the individuals who are employed as advocates are aware of these publications. If they have not been trained in the use of these publications, it is most likely they will not have the regulations, statutes, *Federal Register* releases, or court decisions available. In some counties, commissioners and administrators give only lip service to the needs of veterans and will do just enough to avoid negative public opinion.

Each state funds and operates a Department of Veterans Services that may be a good source for obtaining copies of the information needed to support your contention that the medical condition in question is service related. However, in many states the state veterans service agency coexists with the VA in the regional office. I would suggest you first visit the regional office reading room before trying to obtain the information from the state office.

INTERNET

If you have access to it, the Internet is a great way to copy the required information needed to perfect your claim. You will find the entire 38 CFR, Title 38 U.S. Code, the *Federal Register* for the past several years, and decisions by the United

States Court of Appeals for Veterans Claims. The VA has also posted decisions of the BVA for 1995 and 2001. By surfing several of the university law libraries on the Web, you will find decisions concerning veterans' cases that received an appellate review.

You can find 38 CFR at the following Web addresses:

http://www.access.gpo.gov/nara/cfr/waisidx_01/
    38cfrv1_01.html and
http://www.access.gpo.gov/nara/cfr/waisidx_01/
    38cfrv2_01.html
http://thomas.loc.gov

The *Federal Register* is available at

Gopher://clio.nara.gov.11/register/toc
http://www.access.gpo.gov/su_doc/aces/aces140.html

Title 38 U.S. Code can be found at

http://uscode.house.gov/title_38.htm
http://www4.law.cornell.edu/uscode/38

Case law can be found at these Internet addresses:

http://www.fedcir.gov (U.S. Court of Appeals for the
    Federal Circuit)
http://www.va.gov/vbs/bva
http://www.vetapp.uscourts.gov (U.S. Court of Appeals
    for Veterans Claims)

OTHER SOURCES

A complete list of all federal government Web servers can be found at *http://www.sbaonline.sba.gov/world/federal-servers. html.* For easy reference, print this sixteen-page list of all government servers and bookmark pertinent sites. This index provides direct links to almost three hundred servers. For example, if you want to go to the U.S. Army server, scroll down the alphabetical listing of server addresses until you reach U.S. Army, then click on it.

To purchase a copy of 38 CFR Volume I and Title 38 U.S. Code, contact the Government Printing Office (GPO) via the Internet. The GPO also offers BVA decisions, 1993–1995, on CD-ROM, as well as an annual subscription service published quarterly on CD-ROM. For the location of the closest government bookstore, go to http://www.access.gpo.gov/su_docs/sale.html.

Although the BVA decisions are not precedent setting, they do provide the basis for a strong supportive argument if your claim is denied for the same reason as a similar denied claim that was appealed and reversed. The second reason for researching this database before filing a claim is to determine some of the most common reasons local regional offices deny claims.

Developing the Basic Elements of a Claim

The next step in the claim process is the gathering of evidence that will substantiate the claim. You must establish four facts: that you were in active service; that an injury or disease did occur on active duty and that the condition was not considered acute and transitory; that you are able to show a direct link between the incident that occurred on active duty and your current medical problem; and that you are currently suffering from the residuals of this service-related medical problem. Until you can address all four elements, the claim is not ready to be submitted.

ELEMENT ONE: PROOF OF SERVICE

When an original claim is filed, the very first task the VA will do is to verify military service. It will want to know the type of discharge granted, the length of service, and the branch of service you were in when the alleged injury or disease occurred. The veteran is responsible for providing a certified document that verifies his active duty status at the time of discharge.

The time at which you were separated from the service will determine which document will be required to support your claim. During and following World War Two (WWII), many service members were issued a document that was a formal certificate of discharge on one side and a summary of the individual's military service on the reverse side. Starting in the early 1950s, upon separation, individuals were issued two documents, one a formal certificate of separation and the other a narrative document attesting to the details of the individual's service known as a DD-214.

The DD-214 is the document the VA wants appended to the original claim. A box can be checked on the formal application for compensation or pension benefits (VA Form 21-526) if a certified copy of a Report of Separation is not appended to the claim. The VA will request a copy of your Report of Separation from the NPRC in St. Louis, Missouri, which will add months to the adjudication process.

A request for a copy of the Report of Separation for each period of service should be filed on an SF-180 and mailed to the National Personnel Records Center (Military Personnel Records Division [MPR]), 9700 Page Avenue, St. Louis, MO 63132-5100. The NPRC will provide a certified copy of your DD-214 or Report of Separation at no charge. If the NPRC is unable to provide a certified copy of your DD-214 or separation record it will provide a Certificate of Service that is acceptable for all VA purposes. However, this document will not contain a summarized account of your military service.

Once you receive a certified copy of the document, take it to the clerk of county court or equivalent in your state and have it entered into the public records. The clerk will photocopy it and enter it into the county archives where it will become a permanent record. The original will remain safe, and any copies made from the original will automatically be certified. The clerk will then return the document provided by the NPRC along with a certified copy. The VA will accept this copy. Do not send an original document to the VA if it can be avoided.

If your records were a casualty of the 1973 fire at the NPRC, the NPRC will provide a certified statement based on information obtained from secondary records such as unit morning reports pay records and unit records. This document will be satisfactory for VA purposes.

There are several sources for obtaining blank SF-180s. Most state and county veterans service offices maintain a supply. Or you can call the local VARO (1-800-827-1000) to request one. If you have access to a computer, the form can be downloaded from *http://www.nara.gov/regional/mprsf180.html*. If none of these sources are available, you can write a letter requesting a copy of your DD-214. The letter must contain the following information: name as recorded on service records; service serial number; date of birth and place of birth; social security number; branch of service and organization assigned to when separated; rank; date entered service; and date of separation.

ELEMENT TWO: PROOF OF
SERVICE OCCURRENCE

The whole claim pivots on several important points. First, it must establish that an injury or disease did in fact take place on active duty as alleged. Next, it must show continuity of treatment for the residuals of the injury or illness from the date of separation to the date the claim is filed. However, if the condition is chronic, then proof of continuity of treatment is not an issue. Last, it must establish that the condition is currently being treated. Detailed discussion of chronicity and continuity of treatment can be found in chapter 1.

ELEMENT THREE: CONTINUITY
OF SYMPTOMATOLOGY

As briefly outlined in chapter 1, a claim for service connection becomes extremely difficult to establish under the rule of continuity of symptomatology when you have been separated from the service for many years. The greater the span between separation from the service and the claim date, the harder it is to successfully satisfy this third element. 38 CFR §3.303(b) states that "continuity of symptomatology is required where the condition claimed is shown not to be chronic or where the diagnosis of chronicity may be legitimately questioned."

To prove continuity of symptomatology, a record of continuous medical treatment must be introduced into evidence showing you were under continuous care for the disability claimed. The key factors you must keep in mind are that an injury or disease must have occurred in the service and that since leaving the service you have been treated for this condition. When a claim is initiated many years after leaving the service, the VA usually assumes that the condition you experienced on active duty was acute and transitory, or that the injury healed with no residual effects. Therefore, your current condition was not service incurred.

You have another obstacle to deal with: how many times must you be treated for a condition before the VA accepts there is continuity of treatment? The regulations are totally silent on this point; thus, it is left up to the individual adjudicator to determine how many times he thinks you should have been treated. Along the same lines, the adjudicator has considerable latitude in deciding whether the first available record is a record of postservice treatment of the alleged disease or injury or whether it is a record of treatment of an unrelated service condition.

Many factors will determine your success in providing proof of continuous treatment for your medical condition. Before filing a claim, answer these questions: Have you moved around a lot since leaving the service? Is your doctor still alive? Did the doctor keep your records or were they destroyed? Did your doctor retire from private practice and, if so, were your records destroyed? Did your doctor sell his medical practice and transfer your records to someone else? How often were you treated for this condition? Does your condition go into long periods of remission between episodes?

Physician Search

Again, we are talking about how long it has been since you were last treated by this physician. If it was within the past five years, the chances of locating your doctor are excellent. However, if you are trying to find a doctor who treated you fifteen or twenty years ago, the task becomes much more difficult. Yet there are several methods of finding a physician. Here are some ways to locate a former doctor:

Reference Books   Reed Reference Publishing Company publishes annual editions of the *Directory of Board-Certified Medical Specialists*. This reference source contains the names of all practicing physicians and is cross-referenced by last name, medical specialty, and geographic location. Almost all public libraries have this reference source. The book can be found in medical school libraries as well.

AMA Website   The AMA maintains a physician locator service available to the general public via the Internet. There are several ways to search the database. The two primary methods are by name or medical specialty. It is quite easy to use and contains information on more than five hundred thousand physicians. To access this site, go to *http://ama-assn.org*.

Department of Professional Licensing   Every state requires its physicians to be licensed to practice medicine. Unfortunately, the name of the agency that monitors physician licenses is not consistent from state to state.

State AMA Chapter   If your former physician is a member of his local state AMA organization, locating him should be easy. However, physicians do not have to belong to the AMA.

Internet White and Yellow Pages   If you know where a doctor lives or where you were last treated, try using InfoSpace, a free service on the Internet that furnishes address and phone numbers for more than two hundred million individuals. Go to http://www.infospace.com. I successfully ran several tests on both the white pages and yellow pages. It's a great way to look up someone's phone number or address without dragging out a twenty-pound phone directory.

ELEMENT FOUR: PROOF CURRENTLY DISABLED

This is a very important element in establishing service connection for a condition that has become disabling years after leaving the service. Before service connection will be granted, you must prove that the disease or injury is currently disabling. If the condition being claimed is in remission or not causing a disabling condition, do not file your claim. You cannot satisfy the fourth element. Your claim will be denied and you would not be able to win an appeal.

Very seldom will the VA adjudicate a claim based solely on a non-VA physician's medical assessment. It has the authority to evaluate your claim without scheduling you for an official VA C&P Examination. If you have a condition that is in remission when you are scheduled for a C&P Examination, notify the VA medical facility and the local regional office of this fact and tell them you want to be examined when the condition is active. Make certain this notice is in writing and that you have taken steps to prevent them from claiming they were never notified of your situation. Read chapter 8 for the best procedures to follow to protect your interest when dealing with the VA.

VA regulations require the medical centers to schedule an evaluation when the condition can be properly evaluated. The United States Court of Appeals for Veterans Claims has issued several binding decisions on this issue. You are entitled to a thorough and contemporaneous evaluation before a decision is rendered.

Sources of Evidence: NPRC

Service health records maintained by the NPRC are divided into two categories. The first group is those health records that are maintained and archived with Official Military Personnel

Files (OMPF). The second group is those inpatient hospital records that are maintained and archived separately in files allocated for hospital records.

OUTPATIENT MEDICAL RECORDS

OMPF files are composed of personal records generated during your period of active duty and outpatient health records, which include all sickcall entries and notations, test results and lab findings, radiological reports, entry physical examinations, annual physical examinations, and separation examinations. These medical records are stored with your service record and personnel file. All these records should be requested from the NPRC using SF-180.

However, beginning on October 16, 1992, the Department of the Army transferred all active duty outpatient medical records of recently separated personnel directly to the VA Records Management Center, St. Louis, Missouri. The Navy followed suit on January 31, 1994, the Marine Corps and Air Force on May 1, 1994, and the Air Force Reserve and Air National Guard on June 1, 1994, for personnel discharged, retired, or separated from active duty. Members of the U.S. Coast Guard continue to request copies of their health records from the NPRC in St. Louis.

If health records (outpatient) are located at the NPRC, mail a request for copies to National Personnel Records Center (MPR), 9700 Page Avenue, St. Louis, MO 63132-5100. For health records transferred directly to the VA Records Management Center or one of its regional storage depots, call 1-800-827-1000 for the exact location of your health records and request current instructions for requesting copies. Warning: do not get talked out of obtaining copies of health records based on a VA counselor's advice that the VA will obtain the records after the claim is filed. The sole purpose of obtaining health records in advance is to determine what evidence is available to support your claim. This is the evidence you must take to your medical specialist for review and evaluation.

INPATIENT HOSPITAL RECORDS

Inpatient hospital records are stored separately from OMPF and outpatient health records. To get a copy of these records you must submit a special request to the NPRC preferably using NA Form 13042, Request for Information Needed to Locate Medical Records.

If you are unable to obtain this form, the following information is essential for the NPRC to help provide a copy of your hospital records: name; serial number; social security number; military hospital where treated; period of hospitalization; and medical problem for which you were hospitalized. When identifying the military hospital, identify the branch of service that administers the hospital care. The National Archive and Records Administration (NARA) archives hospital records under the name of the military hospital and branch of service. If you were hospitalized more than once in different military hospitals, each hospital must be identified and pertinent information provided for each period of hospitalization.

TEN MILLION MEDICAL RECORDS DISCOVERED

In 1988, it was announced that a collection of computer tapes containing ten million hospital/treatment facility admissions was discovered by the National Academy of Sciences in one of its storage sites. These records were turned over to the NPRC (MPR) and for the next two years, the archivist decoded the content of these records. When the decoding process was completed, nearly 7.8 million individual admission records were transcribed. The transcription of nearly three-fourths of these coded records is a major medical supplement source of information available to some veterans whose health records were destroyed by fire in 1973 (the remaining one-fourth could not be transcribed).

The admission records are not specific or detailed medical documents, but are simply a summarization of medical information indexed by military service numbers. They contain only limited medical treatment information, but diagnosis, type of operation, and dates and places of treatment or hospitalization are frequently included. The information contained in these files would be sufficient for a veteran to reopen a claim that was previously denied.

The U.S. Army Surgeon General conducted a statistical study on active duty Army and Army Air Corps personnel in service between 1942 and 1945. In addition, active duty Army personnel and a limited number of Marine, Air Force, Navy, and military cadet personnel who served between 1950 and 1954 were also included.

If you were hospitalized during any of the periods mentioned above, request a copy of the medical information recorded from these files from the NPRC (MPR) on an SF-180. In Section II, provide your serial number, the name of the hospital and dates of confinement if possible, and the reason for being an inpatient.

1973 FIRE AT THE NPRC—RECORDS DESTROYED

On July 12, 1973, a disastrous fire at the NPRC (MPR) destroyed 16 to 18 million OMPF. The primary area of destruction was Army and Air Force records. Those individuals in the

Army who were discharged or separated after November 1, 1912, and before January 1, 1960, suffered approximately an 80 percent loss. Air Force personnel who separated or were discharged between September 25, 1947, to January 1, 1964, experienced a 75 percent loss of records. The NPRC determined that the Air Force files that were destroyed started after the name Hubbard James E.

The real tragedy was that the NPRC neither maintained duplicates nor kept microfilm versions of those records destroyed by fire. The problem was further compounded by the fact that before the fire, an index of the records was never compiled. However, the NPRC (MPR) will attempt to reconstruct basic service information when requested by a veteran by using secondary or alternate sources of information. It is not able to reconstruct medical information that was destroyed by the fire.

CASE LAW CONCERNING LOST OR DESTROYED RECORDS

In *O'Hare v. Derwinski, 1 Vet. App. 365 (1991)* and *Sussex v. Derwinski, 1 Vet. App. 526 (1991)*, the United States Court of Appeals for Veterans Claims ruled that when records entrusted to the government are lost or destroyed, special consideration is required. Associate Judge Steinberg, writing for the court in *Sussex v. Derwinski,* states, "bare conclusions as was stated here, that the 'benefit of doubt' doctrine does not apply, is inadequate" (*Gilbert v. Derwinski, 1 Vet. App. at 59*). This inadequacy is more pronounced in light of the BVA's heightened obligation to carefully consider the "Doctrine of Reasonable Doubt" due to the unavailability of the veteran's service medical records. Judge Steinberg, writing in *O'Hare v. Derwinski,* stated,

Here the BVA decision treats the "Doctrine of Reasonable Doubt" rule standard in only the most conclusory terms: '[t]he Doctrine of Reasonable Doubt has been considered, but the evidence is not found to be so evenly balanced as to warrant allowance of the claim.' That is not enough. *This is especially so in a case where the service medical records are presumed destroyed* [emphasis added]; in such a case, the BVA's obligation to explain its findings, conclusions, and to consider carefully the "Doctrine of Reasonable Doubt" rule is heightened.

GETTING COPIES OF HEALTH RECORDS FROM THE NPRC

Requests for military service and health records from the NPRC (MPR) should be submitted on an SF-180. The veteran must state in detail exactly what he is requesting. The NPRC has at times furnished a complete copy of the veteran's service record on microfilm, requiring the records to be photoprocessed before they could be evaluated and possibly used as supporting evidence. Inpatient hospital records are requested separately using SF-180. Failure to provide sufficient information to allow a search of archive records will result in excessive unnecessary delays and archivists sending you NPRC NA Form 13042 to identify the records requested.

WHAT YOU MUST ASK FOR

When requesting copies of service records or medical records from the NPRC (MPR) in St. Louis, use the prescribed form SF-180. The information you are requesting should be stated in Section II, Information and/or Documents Requested, as briefly as possible. For example: "Please provide a copy of all military outpatient health records and a copy of all those records that comprise my personnel file." The other entries on the form will provide the NPRC with all the facts necessary to locate your records.

When requesting inpatient hospital records, an SF-180 should be used. However, a second sheet will probably be necessary to include all the required information. Unlike outpatient records, which are filed with service records, hospital records are archived separately. The searchers must know which hospital you were in, the month and year you were admitted and released, and the nature of the illness, injury, or treatment. When identifying the hospital, the name, numerical designation, and location are essential. Here is an example of how to request copies of multihospitalization inpatient records:

1. "I was admitted to 354th Field Hospital, Columbia, SC, on January 1, 1990, for suspected heart disease. I was discharged from the hospital on January 20, 1990. A triple bypass surgery was performed on January 2, 1990."

2. "On August 15, 1993, I was hospitalized at MacDill Air Force Regional Hospital, Tampa, FL, for acute angina pains. I underwent double bypass surgery on August 16, 1993. I was released on September 10, 1993. Dr. Raymond Jones, Major, USAF, followed me for six months as an outpatient in the cardiology clinic.

Sources of Evidence: VA

You must consider several factors before requesting the VA to provide copies of medical records. The first question you must ask yourself is "Where were my active duty medical files sent after I left the service?" The second question is "How do I get copies of my health records?" The third question is "What do I ask for?" The answers to the above questions will determine which functions within the VA to contact.

WHERE ARE THE RECORDS?

If you filed a previous claim with the VA, request copies of records from the VARO that adjudicated your last claim action. If you were discharged, separated, or retired from the Army after October 1992, or the Navy, Marines, or Air Force after 1994, contact the VA at 1-800-827-1000 for the location of your records within the VA archive system.

If your claim is an original claim, your medical records may be in one of two locations. First, if during outprocessing it was indicated a compensation claim would be filed, the outpatient health records would have been sent to the VARO closest to the address given as a postservice residence.

Next, if no claim action after separation was indicated, the records would be forwarded to one of two places (and you would be notified during outprocessing where they were sent). For separations before October 1992 for Army personnel and January or May 1994 for Navy, Marines, and Air Force, the health records were sent to the NPRC (MPR) in St. Louis, Missouri, for storage. For separations after these dates, health records were transferred to the VA Records Management Center, St. Louis, Missouri, or one of its satellite storage facilities.

A claim action for any other purpose requires you to contact the VARO that was custodian of the claim file. This is a very important step for any veteran who is going to request an action to reopen a previously denied claim; to amend the original claim to include additional disabilities; or to request an increase to an existing disability rating. This is a step that must be taken.

Preparing a claim without knowing exactly what evidence the VA has in your file is inviting a denial of benefits.

When a request is made for a copy of the claim file under the provisions of the Freedom of Information Act, ask for a copy of all the documents, medical records, rating decisions, C&P Examinations results, AMIE instructions to the C&P examining facility, VA Forms 626 (Remarks by Accredited Representatives), and military health records that comprise your file. To plan a winning strategy, you must know what the VA knows and what new or additional evidence will be necessary to support a claim.

HOW DO I GET COPIES OF VA RECORDS?

Military health records maintained by local VAROs are requested by using VA Form 21-4138. It's important to spell out exactly what you want. For active duty health records forwarded to the VA Records Management Center, St. Louis, Missouri, first contact the center by phone at 1-314-263-2800 to find out if your records are located at the St. Louis storage site or at one of the other federal storage depositories.

Outpatient or inpatient medical treatment records stored at a VA medical center or clinic should be requested using VA Form 21-4138. Make certain that the request clearly states exactly what you want. No justification is required to be given before copies of the records will be released. Do not make the assumption that treatment records or inpatient hospital records are automatically forwarded to the local regional office's adjudication division to be placed in your claim file. This does not happen. Adjudicators will not ask medical facilities if they have any hospital or treatment records pertaining to your medical problems unless the veteran has advised them that they exist.

WHAT TO ASK FOR

When requesting copies of records from the Department of Veterans Affairs, the most acceptable way is to state your request on VA Form 21-4138. This form may be used when requesting copies of information from your claim file or when requesting copies of treatment records from a VA medical center or clinic.

I would suggest wording similar to the following when requesting copies of records from a regional office:

> Under the provisions of the Freedom of Information Act, I request a copy of my claim file to include all rating decisions, C&P Examinations, AMIE request to the C&P coordinator at the VA hospital, VA Form 626 filed by my accredited representative when he reviewed the rating decisions, military health records, and all responses from my private physicians.

When requesting copies of medical treatment records from a VA medical center or clinic, follow this example:

> Please provide me with copies of all inpatient and outpatient medical records currently on file at Grand Junction VAMC, Colorado, to include outpatient treatment records, admission history and physical exam reports, operation reports, discharge summaries, progress notes, nursing notes, consultation sheets, lab reports, radiological and imaging reports, and a list of medication prescribed by VA physicians. This information is requested under the provisions of the Freedom of Information Act.

Finally, make a copy of all requests to the VA and NPRC for records. Chapter 8 discusses the safest way to transmit your request for records. You must always back up everything when dealing with these agencies. If the VA lost your request, it may claim that it was never sent and you could lose thousands of dollars because you could not prove it lost your correspondence. I've had several cases where the NPRC (MPR) advised a veteran his health records were destroyed in the 1973 fire; however, the same request was resubmitted through our local congressman's office and soon copies of records allegedly destroyed by the fire magically appeared. Don't always accept responses at face value—check and recheck.

Sources of Evidence: Military Medical Facilities

The medical facility's records administrator will advise you if the records are still under its control or if they were transferred to the NPRC (MPR) and, if so, when. Retired military personnel who received outpatient or inpatient treatment from one of the many military hospitals or clinics around the world have a valuable source of medical evidence to support their claim. Remember that records stored at the NPRC (MPR) in St. Louis are active duty records. Medical records generated at a military installation after leaving active duty are archived by the military until the file has been inactive for several years. Some record collections date back to the 1940s and 1950s, but more comprehensive information was archived beginning in the 1960s. Retiree health records are sent to the NPRC (MPR) from facilities of all military services after one to three years of inactivity and are retained by the NPRC (MPR) for fifty years from the last patient activity. If the date of last treatment at a military facility was less than three years ago, the retiree's first inquiry for copies of health records should be to the facility that provided the treatment.

Sources of Evidence: Nonmedical

Nonmedical evidence can tip the scales in your favor. Nonmedical evidence includes information abstracted from official military historical records, sworn statements from individuals who have personal knowledge of an injury or disease that now is disabling you, BVA decisions, United States Court of Appeals for Veterans Claims decisions, published medical theses by specialists in a specific field of medicine, and VA doctors' qualifications made available by the AMA. Also, spouses, family, and friends can offer testimony as to your well-being before and after leaving the service.

Three quick points: a sworn statement is evidence and has to be weighted with all the facts of the claim; lay statements cannot relate medical opinions but they can relate observations; to rebut these statements the VA has to have evidence to the contrary other than its own unsubstantiated conclusions. The Internet is also a great place to seek out supportive evidence to build a winning claim. Look in chat rooms, veterans bulletin boards, and government servers such as those of the Army, Navy, Marine, and Air Force as well as the Centers for Disease Control and National Science Center.

NATIONAL ARCHIVE RECORDS

A significant portion of historical documents concerning military information is housed in the National Archives Building on Pennsylvania Avenue in Washington, D.C., and the National Archives at College Park, Maryland. Tracking vital information that would support your claim does not require you to go to the nation's capital to visit the National Archives. Since 1969, NARA has managed a system of regional archives that hold valuable federal records of regional origin and significance.

Federal records may also be found in each of the presidential libraries managed by NARA and in a few non-NARA repositories that, by special agreement with the archivist of the United States, are affiliates in the federal network. Contact can be established by mail, telephone, or e-mail in most cases.

The NARA system of archiving documents and records for all government agencies is based on a numerical system of categories. There are more than five hundred primary groups and within each primary group are one hundred subgroups that are further subdivided into twenty or more separate topics. Each of these secondary divisions may have hundreds of actual records. The master index and subdivision index for each record group can be searched on the Internet at *http://www.nara.gov/regional/mpusers.html.*

The following example demonstrates how historical records might prove a veteran's entitlement to VA benefits for diagnosed posttraumatic stress disorder (PTSD). By obtaining copies of key organizational documents from NARA that substantiate the events that caused PTSD, the veteran improved the probability of being granted benefits by 1,000 percent.

Let's say our veteran has access to a computer with a modem. He searches for proof that he suffered a psychological trauma by contacting the NARA gopher site. He is looking for organizational records to substantiate his claim that he experienced a psychological experience so terrible that he is now totally disabled by PTSD.

First, here are the personal facts the VA has on Veteran Jones who served in the Army Air Force during WWII. Sergeant Jones was assigned to 343d Bomb Group, Eighth Air Force, in England, between 1943 and 1945 as an aircraft mechanic. The service information obtained by the VA does not show that on September 19, 1944, he volunteered to fly a B-17 combat mission over Germany, nor do his service medical records reflect any injuries or illnesses while in England. Because the assigned flight engineer/gunner was injured on the previous mission, a temporary engineer/gunner replacement was needed for the forthcoming mission. Military personnel service records of Sergeant Jones do not note any combat duty during his two years overseas.

Veteran Jones logged onto the NARA site (*http://www.nara. gov/research/bytopic/wwii.html*) and clicked on "The Research Room." He scrolled down the next page and clicked "More," which took him to "Research by Selected Topic." He clicked on "World War II: Selected Finding Aids." This took him to "Finding Aids Across NARA Relevant to World War II Records." He then scrolled down and clicked "Military Agency Records Groups." Then he scrolled down to and clicked "Army Air Force (1903-64) RG-13." "Records of the Army Air Force (AAF) Record Group 18, 1903-1964," a general index of files related to the Air Force, opened. He scrolled down the list and clicked on "18.7.1. Records of the Office of the Commanding General." This takes him to a screen that lists all the records maintained for this group.

The veteran mailed his request to Textual Archives Services Division, National Archives, 8601 Adelphi Road, College Park, MD 20740-6001. He also could have called in his request (301-713-7250) or e-mailed it (inquire@nara.gov).

MILITARY HISTORICAL ARCHIVES

Special records on each branch of service are kept by the Department of Defense. Each service branch maintains a military history center. They are an excellent source of information about the history and mission of each organization within a branch of service. For a starting point in collecting information concerning a former organization you may have served in, contact one of the following:

Department of the Navy
9th and M Streets S.E.
Washington, D.C. 20374
202-433-3396 (Personal Papers Collection)
202-433-3439 (Archives Section)
http://www.history.usmc.mil/

U.S. Army Center of Military History
ATTD: DAMH-MD
103 Third Avenue
Ft. McNair, DC 20319-5058
202-761-5373
202-761-5444 (fax)
http://www.armyhistoryfnd.org/info.htm

Air Force History Support Office
AFHSO/HOS
Reference and Analysis Division
200 McChord Street, Box 94
Bolling AFB, DC 20332-1111
http://www.airforcehistory.hq.af.mil/

Naval Historical Center
Washington Navy Yard
805 Kidder Breese Street SE
Washington Navy Yard, DC 20374-5060
http://www.history.navy.mil/

U.S. Marine Corps
Reference Section
Marine Corps Historical Center
Building 58
Washington Navy Yard
Washington, DC 20374-5060

U.S. Army
Attn.: DAMH-ZAX
U.S. Army Center of Military History
103 Third Avenue
Ft. McNair, DC 20319-5058

U.S. Air Force
Air Force Support Office
500 Duncan Avenue, Box 94
Bolling AFB, DC 20332-1111
202-404-2264

U.S. Navy
Naval Historical Center
Washington Navy Yard
901 M Street SE
Washington, DC 20374-5060

Let me give you an example of why knowing where and how to find collaborative evidence is important in the preparation of a claim. Let's assume for the purpose of this illustration that our veteran was a former Navy fireman, serving on the destroyer USS *Macky* during WWII. In 1992, Veteran Smith was diagnosed with lung disease caused by asbestos, forty-five years after he was discharged from the Navy.

Historical facts about the USS *Macky* are needed to build a well-grounded claim that is plausible and not speculative. These are the facts about the ship's combat history obtained from the U.S. Navy Historical Center. The USS *Macky* was severely damaged by a Japanese kamikaze attack. Belowdecks, where our veteran was stationed, many of the steam and electrical wire pipes were destroyed, spewing asbestos dust and particles in all the work and berthing areas aboard ship. For more than three weeks the crippled ship slowly made its way back to Pearl Harbor for repairs. For the next two months the crew worked with civilian shipworkers making internal and external repairs. Asbestos particles filled the air as the damaged areas belowdecks were gutted.

The veteran's personal service records do not mention that the enemy damaged his ship or that the entire crew was exposed to large concentrations of asbestos fibers. Yet fifty years later, the veteran is seriously disabled by asbestosis. The USS *Macky* combat damage can be confirmed by official naval combat records at the Navy Historical Center. Information about the use of asbestos as protective wrapping of piping and fireproofing aboard ship can also be authenticated.

By appending this unimpeachable evidence to his claim, to deny the claim the VA has to prove that such an event did not happen and that nearly three months of exposure to high concentrations of asbestos particles was not sufficient to cause the veteran's disability. This claim is very winnable and is a good example of what doing your homework beforehand and taking charge mean.

SPECIAL MILITARY ARCHIVE SEARCHES

Morning Report

If you are trying to establish proof of an assignment in which exposure to herbicide agents is alleged, copies of the unit morning report should be requested if you served in Vietnam prior to 1974. Any change in a person's duty status is recorded in the daily morning report, including temporary duty assignments, school assignments, changes in occupational specialty, hospitalization, and departing or returning from leave status. Each day through 1974, military personnel, regardless of branch of service, were accounted for by means of the morning report. Subsequent reporting of these data was on personal data cards (PDCs). Both forms of information are in the custody of the NPRC.

Unit Historical Records 1939–1954

Military Unit Operational Records between 1939 and 1954 and between 1954 and the present for units that served in Southeast Asia are located in Archives II Textual Reference Branch, National Archive and Records Administration, 8601 Adelphi Road, College Park, MD 20740-6001.

Unit Historical Records 1954 to Present

Unit Operational Records from 1954 to the present for units that did not serve in Southeast Asia and Organizational History Files 1955 through 1979 are located in the Freedom of Information Act and Privacy Division, Hoffman Building I, Room 1146, 2461 Eisenhower Avenue, Alexandria, VA 22331-0301.

Organizational History Files 1980 to Present

The organizational history of a military unit is available through the U.S. Army Center of Military History, 103 Third Avenue, Ft. McNair, DC 20319-5058. Unofficial material such as unit histories, personal papers, diaries, and photographs including certain select official papers can be obtained from the U.S. Army Institute of Heraldry, 9325 Gunston Road, Room S-112, Fort Belvoir, VA 22060-5579.

Radiation Exposure Records

A copy of service personnel records confirming unit of assignment, location and dates of assignment, military service number, and military occupational specialty when exposed to radiation is necessary to initiate a search of radiation exposure records. Another source of supportive evidence confirming the same information found in service records is the unit morning report.

Outpatient Medical Records   Copies of outpatient medical records should be obtained as a possible source of evidence of radiation exposure. Copies can be requested by submitting an SF-180 to the NPRC (MPR), 9600 Page Avenue, St. Louis, MO 63132-5100. Send a separate request for each record group as various archival departments are involved.

Defense Special Weapons Agency   The Defense Special Weapons Agency (DSWA), formerly the Defense Nuclear Agency, manages the Nuclear Test Personnel Review (NTPR) program for the Department of Defense. Through the NTPR program, veterans may learn the details of their individual participation and their radiation doses, obtain documentation about the tests, and learn their organization's mission in atmospheric testing or occupational duty.

This agency has extensive archival records about various Army, Air Force, Navy, and Marine Corps organization's participation in U.S. atmospheric tests conducted from 1945 to 1962. The agency has identified nearly 210,000 individuals who were participants in atmospheric testing. DSWA has also identified another 195,000 individuals who were members of occupational forces of Hiroshima and Nagasaki, Japan. Another key function of this agency is to collect and analyze sources of recorded dosimetry and radiation data. DSWA will provide calculated doses in cases where recorded doses are unavailable or incomplete.

All requests for documents establishing proof of participation in a foreign government's nuclear tests must state that the request deals with non-U.S. test participation. Proof of participation can be obtained from the following Department of Defense sources:

U.S. Air Force
Commander, Nonflight Duties
Department of the Air Force
Armstrong Laboratory
AL/OEBS, Bldg. 140
Brooks AFB, TX 78235-5500
410-536-2378

U.S. Air Force
HQAFTAC/ICO
Flight Missions
1030 South Highway A1A
Patrick AFB, FL 32925-3002
407-494-6867

U.S. Army
Chief, U.S. Army Ionizing Radiation Dosimetry Center
ATTN.: AMXTM-SR-D
PO Box 14063
Lexington, KY 40512-4063
606-293-3646

U.S. Coast Guard
Commandant (G-KSE)
U.S. Coast Guard
2100 2nd Street SW
Washington, DC 20593
202 267-1368

U.S. Navy and U.S. Marine Corps
Officer in Charge
Naval Dosimetry Center
Navy Environmental Health Center Detachment
Bethesda, MD 20889-5614
301-295-5426

Ionizing Radiation Records

Morning Report If you are trying to establish proof of an assignment in which exposure to ionizing radiation is alleged, copies of the unit morning report should be requested from the NPRC (MPR).

Unit Historical Records 1939–1954 Military Unit Operational Records between 1939 and 1954 and between 1954 and the present for units that served in Southeast Asia are located at Archives II Textual Reference Branch, National Archive and

Records Administration, 8601 Adelphi Road, College Park, MD 20740-6001.

Unit Historical Records 1954 to Present   Unit Operational Records from 1954 to the present for units that did not serve in Southeast Asia and Organizational History Files from 1955 through 1979 are located at the Freedom of Information Act and Privacy Division, Hoffman Building I, Room 1146, 2461 Eisenhower Avenue, Alexandria, VA 22331-0301.

Organizational History Files 1980 to Present   The organizational history of a military is available through the Army Center of Military History, 103 Third Avenue, Ft. McNair, DC 20319-5058.

Unofficial Unit Records   Unofficial material such as unit histories, personal papers, diaries, and photographs, including certain select official papers, can be obtained from the U.S. Army Institute of Heraldry, 9325 Gunston Road, Room S-112, Fort Belvoir, VA 22060-5579.

Exposure to Radiation Documents

Each branch of service maintains a record of occupational radiation exposure. If your request for a copy of DD-1141, Record of Occupational Exposure to Ionizing Radiation, from the NPRC is not fruitful, follow up with a request to the appropriate branch of service. The following identifying data must be included in your request for a copy of DD-1141: name; current address and telephone number; social security number; VA claim number if one is assigned from a previous claim; service number; period of service; date and place of birth; and nature of your disability. The addresses for the branches of service are as follows:

U.S. Air Force
Department of the Air Force
USAF Occupational Health Laboratory (AFSC)
Brooks AFB, TX 78235-5501

U.S. Army
Chief, U.S. Army Ionizing Radiation Dosimetry Center
ATTN.: AMXTM-CE-DCR
Lexington, KY 40511-5102
606-239-3249

U.S. Coast Guard
Commandant
U.S. Coast Guard
ATTN.: Mr. James Veazey
2100 2nd Street SW
Washington, DC 20593-0001

U.S. Navy and U.S. Marine Corps
Officer in Charge
Naval Dosimetry Center
Navy Environmental Health Center
Bethesda, MD 20889-5614
301-295-5426

Office of Human Radiation Experiments
The Office of Human Radiation Experiments (OHRE) is a function assigned to the secretary for Environment, Safety and Health under the Department of Energy. This office has located,

identified, and uncovered nearly four thousand human radiation experiments by the federal government between 1944 and 1974. Direct your inquires to Department of Energy-OHRE (EH-8), 1000 Independence Avenue SW, Washington, DC 20585; 202-586-8800.

Sources of Evidence: Witnesses

Sworn statements from you, family, friends, and former "buddies" are hard evidence that the VA must consider and weigh during the adjudication process. A statement from a third party (lay evidence) when properly executed is very important in the adjudication process. It is just as important as service medical records, postservice doctor's assessments, or any other form of evidence when building a well-grounded claim.

Until the United States Court of Appeals for Veterans Claims became a reality on October 16, 1989, such statements, for all practical purposes, were worthless. In most cases the VA adjudicators simply ignored sworn statements and in others they refused to explain why a sworn statement was not relevant and supportive of the veteran's claim. It can be safely assumed that the VA considered these statements as self-serving and of questionable veracity. However, the court, in deciding *Caluza v. Brown, 7 Vet. App. 498 (1995)*, again narrowed the powers of the VA in deciding issues involving lay evidence. The decision reminded the VA that 38 U.S.C.A. §5107(a) states that "Truthfulness of evidence is presumed in determining whether a veteran's claim is well-grounded."

In 1991, the court decided several more similar cases in favor of the veteran. In *Hamlets v. Derwinski, 1 Vet. App. 164 (1991)*, the court stated that the BVA *must* explain why it did not accept the credibility of the appellant's personal sworn testimony as evidence. *Cartright v. Derwinski, 2 Vet. App. 24 (1991)* followed this decision in December 1991, stating "the Secretary cannot ignore the appellant's testimony simply because the appellant is an interested party." The decision went on to point out that the VA *cannot* treat a veteran's sworn statement only as part of his contention; *"[I]t must account for and explain its reasons for rejecting the testimony* [emphasis added]."

WAYS TO SEARCH FOR WITNESSES

Finding people is no longer an impossible task, especially if you have certain basic facts. To get started you need minimum background information about the individual such as complete name, where they were from, military unit you were both assigned to, rank, and military specialty. The more personal information you have about an individual, the quicker your search will turn up your witness. In today's world you have at your disposal many different government archives, the Internet, veterans organizations, and commercial research businesses that for a price will find anyone. Finding a witness is no longer an impossible task even if fifty years have passed since your last meeting.

Computer Search for Friends and Buddies

The Internet is an excellent place to start your search for a former friend or relative. Almost all public libraries make computers available to its patrons. Three separate search services can be used: bulletin boards, the Web, and newsgroups.

Some bulletin boards are specifically dedicated to veterans and military such as Prodigy, America Online, and MSN. To access these bulletin boards, you must pay a monthly fee for service from one of these providers. Regarding Internet newsgroups, several sites can be used to locate individuals:

- sci.military.naval
- sci.military.moderated
- soc.veterans
- soc.historywar.world-II
- soc.history.war.vietnam

Another valuable source on the Internet is search engines. These search services make available more than two hundred million telephone numbers and addresses. Many services supply the individual's e-mail address as well. There is no charge for the use of these search engines. The primary search engines are

- Yahoo's People Search (http://www.yahoo.com)
- Excite's People Finder (http://www.excite.com)
- Big Yellow's Find People (http://wp.bigyellow.com)
- Google (http://www.google.com/advanced_search)
- WhoWhere? (http://www.whowhere.com)
- Anywho (http://www.anywho.com)
- Netscape's People (http://www.netscape.com; click on White Pages in header)

In addition, commercial services on the Internet specialize in locating individuals for a fee. One such service (http://www.1800ussearch.com/usProduct.html) uses the social security number to provide all current and past addresses for the past seven to ten years. In addition to providing telephone number, date of birth, any known aliases, name variations, and state and year this social security number was issued, this service responds within 24 hours by e-mail or fax. The cost is $40 per name, and $12 to $100 for various other searches.

If you kept a copy of all orders issued throughout your service period, you might have a source of vital information that will help you locate a former comrade. You will have a complete name and either a service number or social security number to start your search.

Government Agencies

U.S. Air Force   The Air Force provides locator service only for officers and airmen on active duty, retirees, reservists, and guardsmen. Other former members of the Air Force or Army Air Corps must be researched using alternate methods. To use this locator service, write Air Force Worldwide Locator, AFPC/MSIMDL, 550 C Street West, Suite 50, Randolph AFB, TX 78150-4752. Or you can speak to a live person at 210-565-2660. The Air Force will not release the location of someone stationed overseas or in a sensitive position. However, it will forward a letter to the individual if the correct postage is on the envelope and any required fee has been paid.

U.S. Army   The Army's policy concerning the release of the last known address of former Army members is strictly prohibited by the Privacy Act of 1974. However, it will assist your search by forwarding your letter to the service member's last known address. To use this service, follow these steps:

1. Place your letter in a sealed, stamped envelope and write your return address in the upper left corner.
2. Write a letter to the NPRC requesting its assistance and provide as much of the following information as possible: the veteran's full name, serial number and/or social security number, and date of birth.
3. Place your sealed envelope to the veteran and the letter

to the NPRC in a second envelope and mail to National Personnel Records Center, 9700 Page Avenue, St. Louis, MO 63132-5100.

U.S. Marine Corps   The Marine Corps does not offer a formal way of contacting former marines. However, it does provide three alternatives. The Corps publishes a monthly magazine entitled *Leatherneck* that offers a special service for locating former marine buddies. Your locator request is similar to the personal columns found in most daily newspapers. At a minimum, the information should include the veteran's full name, the unit you both served in, the period you were assigned together, a reason for trying to locate him, and your complete return address.

The second contact method is via the Internet on a Web page known as "Lost Buddies" (*http://www.pos.net/Marine/lostbuds.html*). Here you can post a message on the Web requesting the location of a former marine. As you read through the messages by other marines, you quickly get the drift of how to look for a lost friend.

The third method available to you is signing onto the Marine Guest Book at *http://www.thefew.com*. A search engine is built into the web page so you can search for a former buddy by last name.

U.S. Navy   Similar to the Air Force, the Navy has two separate programs, one for individuals on active duty and another for those who have retired. Family members, active duty personnel, and retirees may use the Navy's *World Wide Locator*. To do so, you need the service member's full name, social security number, grade or rank, and, if possible, last known duty station. Address your letter to *World Wide Locator*, Bureau of Naval

Personnel, Per-312, 5700 Integrity Drive, Millington, TN 38053-3120.

When trying to locate a navy retiree through the *World Wide Locator*, follow the same four steps outlined under the U.S. Army with one exception: send your letter to the address given in the preceding paragraph.

Department of Veterans Affairs   You may be able to locate a former comrade using the VA. The first step is to call the local regional office servicing your state at 1-800-827-1000 to determine if the veteran is in its database. If so, the VARO will likely have a valid address for the individual. The telephone counselor will instruct you in the proper way to prepare the letter you wish to have forwarded on your behalf. The method used when working through the VA is similar to that outlined above for the remailing service offered by the U.S. Army. In this case you address your cover letter to the local regional office asking that it forward your unaddressed letter to the veteran. Again, being able to provide a service number or social security number will better your chances of a successful contact.

Department of State   A source often overlooked in a search for a former friend is the U.S. Department of State. Many former service personnel reside in foreign countries after leaving the military. An American citizen residing in a foreign country must register with the U.S. Embassy or Consulate. U.S. embassies and consulates help locate U.S. citizens overseas for relatives or friends. The Department of State estimates that it handles over two hundred thousand such requests each year.

Persons in the United States inquiring about the whereabouts of a citizen abroad may contact the Department of State, Overseas Citizens Services, by phone at 1-202-647-5225. If you wish to write for assistance in locating a former service member residing overseas, address your letter to Overseas Citizens Services, U.S. Department of State, 2201 C Street NW, Washington, DC 20520. In your letter or conversation with a representative of the Department of State, tell them you need to locate your friend so he can provide vital testimony that will have a positive effect on the outcome of a claim pending before the VA.

Newspaper/Magazines

Newspaper Classifieds   This is an excellent method to use if your former comrade was from a large metropolitan area such as New York, St. Louis, San Francisco, Los Angeles, Detroit, Chicago, Houston, or Dallas. Each of these cities has more than one daily paper. Obtain the name of the paper, mailing address, and phone numbers through your local library's reference department. Placing a short message in the classified personal section may lead to a contact. The ad should be brief and contain just enough basic information so the individual would recognize that he is being sought.

If you are trying to locate an individual who is still on active duty, place a classified ad in any one of the service newspapers. The Times Publishing Company publishes four special weekly editions of its newspaper, one for each branch of service: the *Army Times, Air Force Times, Navy Times,* and *Marine Corps Times.* The *Stars and Stripes*, a 130-year-old newspaper, is published overseas for American military personnel stationed outside the continental United States; the domestic edition is dedicated to veterans of all wars. The *Stars and Stripes* is an excellent newspaper source to locate individuals stationed overseas or veterans in the United States.

To contact these newspaper publishing companies, write as follows:

Army Times Publishing Company, Inc.
Classified Department
6883 Commercial Drive
Springfield, VA 22159
703-750-8915
http://www.atpco.com

Stars & Stripes
Business Office
PO Box 187
Thurmont, MD 21788
http://www.estripes.com

For example, the ad might read as follows: Looking for Henry B. Wall, a former marine Sgt. from VFM 126, aboard the USS *George Washington,* between April 1, 1990, and August 3, 1994. Urgent! Please reply to: John Paul Jones, Box 2210, Shreveport, LA 37802-2210.

You might want to rent a mailbox through the post office or a private business to forestall annoying mail predators who load you with uninvited junk offers. This way you can throw away all the junk mail at the post office and your actual address will be protected.

Magazines   Monthly and bimonthly magazines published by the various service organizations may offer a better opportunity to reach a former service person if you have no idea where he may reside. On the other hand, newspaper classifieds are an excellent search tool for locating someone if you have a general idea of where to look.

Veterans service organizations have millions of members who receive their monthly magazine as part of their membership package. Many of these same organizations have their own website and offer various online services to both members and nonmembers.

Dozens of monthly or bimonthly magazines are dedicated to veterans and active duty personnel. Most associations formed during the 1970s, 1980s, and 1990s as well as those whose roots go back before the turn of the twentieth century publish their own organizational magazine for the benefit of their membership. The service organization magazines are too numerous to include them all. Here are just a few of the organizations whose membership reach into the millions:

American Legion Magazine
Advertising Editor Assistance
PO Box 1055
Indianapolis, IN 46206
http://www.legion.org/publications/pubs_mag_index.htm
317-630-1200

V.F.W. Magazine
Advertising Editor
Veterans of Foreign Wars Building
406 West 34th Street, Suite 219
Kansas City, MO 64111
http://www.vfw.org/magazine/
816-756-3390

DVA Magazine
Department of Veterans Affairs
PO Box 14301
Cincinnati, OH 45250-0301
http://www.dav.org/magazine

NCOA Journal
Noncommissioned Officers Association
1065 IH 35N
San Antonio, TX 78233
http://www.ncoausa.org
1-800-662-2620

Retired Officer Magazine
Editor
The Retired Officers Association
201 N. Washington Street
Alexandria, VA 22314
http://www.troa.org; *http://www.troa.org/Locator/Default.asp*
703-683-1480

Naval Affairs
ATTN: Editor
Fleet Reserve Association
125 N. West Street
Alexandria, VA 22314-2754
http://www.fra.org/navalaffairs/

Leatherneck
Mail Call Editor
PO Box 1775
Quantico, VA 22134
http://www.mca-marines.org/Leatherneck/lneck.html

Air Force Magazine
Air Force Association
1501 Lee Highway
Arlington, VA 22209-1198
http://www.afa.org/magazine/magz.html
703-247-5800

National Archives

Most people never have a need to use the services offered by NARA. Yet it is one of the most valuable sources of obtaining primary and secondary evidence to support a claim for compensation benefits. The secret is to know what information to ask for and where to address your inquiry.

In most cases, large agencies such as the Department of Defense store their historical records first by branch of service, then subdivided by various commands, headquarters, and organizational units. NARA has two primary storage facilities and twelve regional centers. Most military information is stored in one of three locations: National Archives I, 700 Pennsylvania Avenue NW, Washington, DC 20408, and National Archives II located at 8601 Adelphi Road, College Park, MD 20740-6001. The third primary location of interest to veterans is the National Personnel Records Center, 9700 Page Avenue, St. Louis, MO 63132-5100. Personnel service records, outpatient health records, and military hospital records are stored at this facility.

A twenty-nine page document entitled "A Citizen's Guide to the Nation's Archives" can be accessed online at http://tis.eh.doe.gov/ohre/roadmap/achre/archives.html. A complete list of government servers on the Web can be downloaded from *http://www.sbaonline.sba.gov/world/federal-servers.html*. This is a terrific index of government agencies that can be contacted via the Internet for vital research information, releasable under the Freedom of Information Act.

Information from the NARA could help you obtain compensation benefits when there are no primary records or documents to support your claim. A case can be built using secondary sources of evidence so that the doctrine of reasonable doubt is triggered in your favor. Background facts of our imaginary case are as follows: You injured your back and hip in March 1974 when you fell off the wing of a KC 135 aircraft you were working on, while stationed at MacDill Air Force Base (AFB), Tampa, Florida. The hospital records could not be located and your outpatient records are silent as to any back or hip problem.

By obtaining a copy of the morning report for your unit for the period you were hospitalized, you can establish that you were in fact hospitalized. The morning report will not explain why you were in the hospital, only that you were a patient. Next, you want to get a copy of the Line of Duty Investigation (LOD) initiated to investigate the incident. This investigative report shows that your injury was in the line of duty and that you did indeed fall off the wing of an airplane. Next, you want to further collaborate this information with a sworn statement from a friend who was with you when you were injured and who visited you several times during your hospitalization. A nurse told Airman Blackburn the extent of your injuries. You located your friend through the NPRC in St. Louis. Your letter was forwarded to him at the address he gave when being discharged. Airman Blackburn, now Mr. Ronald Blackburn of Tampa, Florida, furnished you with a sworn **affidavit**. You also prepared a sworn statement detailing the events of the injury, your hospitalization, symptoms you experienced, when they started, and all postservice medical treatment for back and hip.

The final step involves showing continuity of treatment for the injury to your hip and back. Having given your orthopedic specialist a copy of all the evidence you obtained and a copy of rating schedule 38 CFR §4.71(a)(5250 and 5293), your doctor wrote that after reviewing the LOD, Mr. Blackburn's sworn statement, your sworn statement, and his examination, tests, and imaging reports, he believed that the accident you had in the service is the cause of the residual problems you are now experiencing. In assessing your current level of disability, your doctor also noted that your condition is characteristic of injuries that occurred many years ago. He should further state that using the VA rating standards outline in 38 CFR Part 4, your hip injury is 70 percent disabling and your back injury is 60 percent disabling.

The VA would be hard pressed to deny this claim because to rebut your evidence it must have substantial evidence to the contrary. All it would have is its own unsubstantiated opinions. A claim carefully crafted like this, even though all the evidence is of a secondary nature, has everything in its favor.

I am not saying that the local regional office might grant benefits based on a first-time review of the evidence and facts. You have to remember that the individual reviewing the claim is not medically trained to comprehend the complexities of any given illness or injury nor is he trained to apply the concepts of law the case is being based on. Furthermore, the rating board member will devote no more than a couple of hours to your claim. He will not spend time researching medical issues he knows very little or nothing about. He won't review the file in its entirety, page by page, or spend time trying to decipher scribbled medical information written by some VA doctor.

You put together a well-grounded claim that will eventually win. If you are satisfied your claim is based on facts and the evidence you based the claim on supports your contentions, *never, never back off and quit in frustration. Appeal! Appeal! Appeal!* Sooner or later your claim will reach a level where an individual is capable of adjudicating the claim based on the laws and medical facts.

Miscellaneous Sources

In tracking a former service member, include state or local government agencies in your search plan. Most states will provide a current address based on a registered driver's license. The more information you provide, the better your chances of receiving helpful information.

The success rate increases if the individual does not have a common name such as Smith, Jones, Brown, or Green. Can you imagine how many Smiths live in New York State? Try to provide the agency with the individual's full name, approximate location of residence, age, and sex. For example, if you knew that your buddy entered the service from Westbury, Long Island, New York, send the initial request to the Department of Motor Vehicles, Empire State Plaza, Albany, NY 12228. Your letter should provide his full name, age, gender, and the city, town, or county he lived in before entering the service.

You can find the correct mailing address and telephone number of the auto licensing agency in your public library's reference department. As most states charge a small fee for this service, call first for the costs and the information they will need.

Several books provide some practical insight as to where to start looking for a lost friend or family member and how to go about it.

- *How to Locate Anyone Who Is or Has Been in the Military: Armed Forces Locator Guide* (8th Ed.) by Richard S. Johnson and Debra Johnson Knox. Spartanburg, SC: Military Information Enterprises, 1999.
- *Find Anyone Fast: By Phone, Fax, Mail and Computer* by Richard S. Johnson and Debra Johnson Knox. Spartanburg, SC: Military Information Enterprises, 2001.

- *How to Find Almost Anyone, Anywhere* by Norma Mott Tillman. Nashville, TN: Rutledge Hill Press, 1995.

Consult your local librarian for other titles that would assist you in your efforts to locate a former buddy.

SWORN STATEMENT BY THE CLAIMANT

When filing an original claim or a claim for increased benefits, amending an original claim, or reopening a previously denied claim, a sworn statement by the claimant should be part of the package. Nowhere in statutes, regulations, or manuals does it state that the VA will ask for a narrative statement detailing the circumstances and limitations imposed by your disability. Yet the records provide only limited facts that will be the basis of the decision.

Medical records and service records provide very little insight as to the actual circumstances surrounding the events responsible for the injury or disease. The records will not provide a clear picture of the ever-present pain and limitations imposed by the injury or disease. The records the VA will work with will not reveal how the current medical problem affects your ability to earn a livable wage, why your employment was terminated, or that you had to quit working because you could no longer function in the workplace.

The problem is further complicated by the fact that the VA maintains a nationwide adjudication force of employees who may have no more than a high school education yet decide complex medical and legal issues. They receive no extensive training in injury or disease medicine so as to properly comprehend the complexities of reported medical problems nor are they provided with formal legal training to enable them to apply the concepts of law created by decisions of the court.

With the VA using single-signature rating by individuals with no formal medical or legal training, you cannot afford to be casual and assuming. You need to submit a claim that is well documented so that if the benefits are denied at the local regional office level and you are forced to appeal, your benefits will eventually be granted.

Until a major change takes place in the adjudication process, background information reported by a physician evaluating your medical condition will be treated as hearsay evidence and dismissed as unsubstantiated. The VA justifies the exclusion of your physician's remarks on the basis the doctor has no factual knowledge of the event and is only reporting what you said. However, with the introduction of sworn testimonies as evidence, the VA must now evaluate and weigh these affidavits with all the other evidence and facts related to the claim; it cannot dismiss them as not factual.

Example of Claimant's Sworn Statement

There is no set format in which to initiate a sworn statement. The sworn testimony is in narrative form and should be typed. The statement should be brief and the language carefully chosen. Base your information only on pertinent facts of the issue under consideration. Your statement should be sworn and signed before a notary public.

I must caution you that a lay statement cannot express a factual opinion concerning a medical issue. Only competent medical personnel can make statements of a factual basis regarding a medical problem.

The following illustration is offered as a guide in organizing your declaration. The contents of your declaration will depend primarily upon the facts you wish to have considered as evidence. This format is very workable and when properly executed is a valuable document.

Declaration of John Paul Jones

Now comes John Paul Jones, being duly sworn, and states as follows:

1. My name is John Paul Jones. I reside at 1421 Riverside Drive, Chicago, IL 20616.
2. I enlisted in the U.S. Navy in October 1952 and served honorably until I was medically discharged on April 20, 1954, for anxiety reaction and moderate chronic depression. When separated I was given disability severance pay in the amount of $7,600.
3. Following my separation I returned to the Chicago area where I was treated at VAMC Hines Mental Health Clinic for approximately three years. The treatment consisted of one-on-one therapy sessions with a psychiatrist. I have tried for several years to retrieve copies of my clinic file for the period 1969 to 1970, to no avail. I've been promised several times by the hospital records department that the records would be obtained from storage, copied, and forwarded to me. To date this has not happened.
4. I received additional treatment from VAMC Hines Mental Health Clinic on an irregular basis for chronic anxiety with depression from 1982 through 1990.
5. Following my medical discharge in April 1954, I have been unable to develop a stable work history. With the exception of one job that lasted three years, the longest I worked for any one employer was one year. In a majority of the cases the reason I was terminated was because I could not get along with other employees or deal with the public without having a sudden response of sudden anger at the slightest provocation. I have not been able to work for the past five years.
6. I'm unable to concentrate at times to the degree that people start looking at me when I do not respond to them appropriately.

> I often have a deep feeling of guilt, and in many cases I am
> unable to determine why I feel guilty. I sleep very poorly and
> wake up many times during the night. I often lie awake for
> hours with the feeling that something terrible is going to happen.
> I have lost more than 40 pounds since leaving the service.
>
> 7. On September 1, 1996, I was granted social security disability
>   benefits for anxiety and depression.
> 8. I declare under the penalty of perjury that the above statement
>   is true and correct to the best of my knowledge.
>
> ---
>
> Date   Signature of John Paul Jones
>
>   Notary Seal and
>   Certification Here

SWORN STATEMENT BY SPOUSE, FAMILY, AND FRIENDS

A spouse, immediate family, or close friends of a veteran can
provide valuable support for a claim by a sworn statement.
The same rules that apply to the veteran also apply to spouses,
family, or friends; for example, they cannot say, "I know that
John P. Jones has a severe anxiety condition." Court decisions
back up regulations and manuals that a layperson is not qualified
to give evidence pertaining to a medical condition. However,
they can give evidence as to what they observed and the circumstances at the time the observation was made.

Example of a Sworn Statement by a Spouse

The following is a suggested format for a spouse, family, or
friend who will give a sworn statement. Again the same basic
rules previously discussed apply in preparing the declaration.

Declaration of Patty Ann Jones

Now comes Patty Ann Jones, being duly sworn, and states as follows:

1. My name is Patty Ann Jones. I am the wife of John Paul Jones. I reside with my husband at 1421 Riverside Drive, Chicago, IL 20616.

2. I have known my husband since January 1971 and married him two years later on June 2, 1973. I have been with my husband every day since 1971 and have observed the effect of his disability on a daily basis.

3. During the past twenty-five years John has had fifteen jobs, which never last more than a year. He has not been employed for the past five years. Several of the jobs he quit; the only explanation he offered was he couldn't get along with the boss. But the majority of times he was terminated because he was disruptive in the workplace and at odds with other employees. He has no close personal friends and will not go out and join in local social events.

4. John has been taking Xanax and Zoloft for several years for anxiety and depression and has been in and out of therapy at Hines VAMC Mental Health Clinic for the past several years.

5. Although he has never been abusive to me physically or verbally, he has flared into a rage when provoked by neighbors or strangers.

6. During the past five years he often was very depressed and slept twelve to fifteen hours a day. Also during these periods he said that he would be better off if he were dead. Once I could get him back to the mental health clinic, they would readjust his medication and his condition would improve.

7. John is always expressing thoughts that reflect fear and hopelessness. He has not shown any interest in participating in hobbies or attending public events; he seems to withdraw from any contact with other people and invents all kinds of excuses for why he must stay away.

8. John was granted social security disability benefits about a year

ago. His award letter stated that the benefits were granted on the basis of severe chronic anxiety and depression.

9. I declare under penalty of perjury that the above is correct to the best of my knowledge.

Date   Signature of Patty Ann Jones

                                        Notary Seal and
                                        Certification Here

SWORN STATEMENT BY EMPLOYERS

A sworn statement from an employer or former employer can influence the rating process. Compensation benefits are supposed to be determined by the degree the disability reduces your capability to be gainfully employed. Unfortunately, obtaining statements from some supervisors or employers may prove very difficult. An employer or former employer may be reluctant to provide a statement of reasons for the veteran's termination. For example, if the veteran had a severe psychological problem the employer may fear for his own and his employees' well-being. An employer who terminates a veteran for physical disabilities risks being sued under the Americans with Disabilities Act. You should be willing to give your former employer a release against any lawsuits and in no way present yourself as a danger to him. In many cases a third party such as a spouse, family member, or friends will be able to negotiate on your behalf.

Example of a Sworn Statement by Employer
The following will provide some guidance in preparing a sworn declaration by a former employer.

Declaration of Henry R. Smith

Now comes Henry R. Smith, being duly sworn, and states as follows:

1. My name is Henry R. Smith and I reside at 5151 Lake Front Circle, Apartment 1121, Chicago, IL 20631.
2. I am the owner of Smith Tool and Die Company, located at 304 Orange Street, Complex D, Chicago, IL 20611. My company subcontracts to many manufacturers for special machine parts for their products.
3. I hired John Paul Jones on June 1, 1991, as a metal lathe operator at a starting salary of $15 per hour. Approximately six months after I hired him his work performance began to change. He had several verbal arguments with another machinist whom I had employed for many years. I counseled him on his workplace behavior. Mr. Jones's attitude with other workers improved but the quality of his performance was poor.
4. Mr. Jones was terminated on May 10, 1992, due to an incident that nearly cost him his left hand. Mr. Jones failed to properly install a clamping chuck for the item he was going to make on the lathe. As a result, his sleeve became snagged by the piece of metal that was about to be turned. His left arm was jerked into the rotating piece of metal stock. Fortunately another worker saw the incident and immediately pushed the emergency shutdown button. This saved Mr. Jones's arm from being severed.
5. I subsequently learned that the VA mental health clinic had put Mr. Jones on Xanax and Zoloft. Both of these medications indicate that patients should not operate machinery.
6. I had no option but to terminate Mr. Jones, for his protection and the protection of my other employees.
7. I declare under the penalty of perjury that the above statement is true and correct to the best of my knowledge.

_____

Date   Signature of Henry R. Smith

> Notary Seal and
> Certification Here

SWORN STATEMENT BY FORMER COMRADES

Letters from former comrades, or buddy letters, are a very valuable source of testimonial evidence in establishing the factual background of an injury or disease. This is especially true when the injury or disease was neither recorded by a medical corpsman nor entered into the claimant's medical file at the time of the incident. In the past, buddy letters were not seriously considered as evidence. The statements were treated as a lie or not having credibility.

I worked a case of a former POW in which all the surviving members of a B-17 bomber attested that the veteran received injuries to his ears as a result of a high altitude bailout when the aircraft was destroyed by flak. Even though the veteran had a severe cold and blocked sinuses, the flight surgeon had refused to ground him. The squadron was ordered to put up a maximum effort and because there were no spare waist gunners, the claimant had no choice but to fly the mission. His buddies all testified that a German doctor treated the veteran for his ear condition. He was told that he had ruptured his eardrums. The crew's statements were not accepted as evidence of his hearing loss because available service medical records were silent as to any hearing problems. The veteran was eventually granted service connection for his hearing loss upon appeal. However, it took five years for the appeal to work its way through the system.

The local regional office had no evidence to contradict the sworn statements of the veteran or his crew other than its own unsubstantiated opinion. As previously stated, a rating board must specifically state what evidence it has that rebuts the sworn statements by the veteran or others. Rating boards must accept sworn statements as credible evidence and must give the evidence equal weight with all the other evidence of record.

Formerly, locating former members of your military unit who had factual information concerning your injury or disease was almost an impossible task. However, beginning in the late 1980s and early 1990s, locating people was no longer an impossible task. Success still depends a great deal on how much you remember about the individual. Thanks to giant advances in storing and retrieving personnel data, locating people is much easier.

At your disposal now are nationwide phone directories; letters forwarded to former buddies by several government agencies; online computer searches through bulletin boards; placement of notices in many of the veterans service organization monthly magazines or publications; reunions held by military organizations; and personal ads in newspapers where the veteran may have resided after leaving the service. Plus, within the past few years many small businesses have surfaced that will find a person for a nominal fee.

Example of a Sworn Buddy Letter

Declaration of Ronald Blackburn

Now comes Ronald Blackburn, being duly sworn, and states as follows:
1. My name is Ronald Blackburn and I reside at 4551 Swan Avenue, Tampa, FL 33603.
2. I served with Sergeant Henry Miller at MacDill Air Force Base, Tampa, FL, between July 1, 1970, and June 30, 1974. We were

both assigned to the 301st Air Refueling Wing's maintenance squadron. Sergeant Miller was discharged in June 1974, and I retired from the Air Force on August 31, 1995, as a Chief Master Sergeant E-9.

3. We were both performing inspections on the upper surface of the left wing of a KC-135 when Sergeant Miller slipped and slid off the leading edge of the wing. When I looked over the edge of the wing, he was lying on his back. He fell approximately twelve feet before striking the cement ramp. The accident happened in early March 1974. The Line Chief Sergeant immediately sounded the alarm for medical care and the base hospital dispatched an ambulance. I recall that Sergeant Miller was hospitalized for nearly two weeks.

4. I visited him several times while he was hospitalized. I was told by the duty nurse during the first visit that although he did not break any bones he did injure his hip and lower back quite seriously. For more than a week they had him heavily sedated because of the pain.

5. When Sergeant Miller was released from the hospital, he was assigned to limited duty status until his discharge on June 30, 1974. He performed no duties that involved lifting or twisting. He was assigned to work in the squadron orderly room running errands for the sergeant major and commander.

6. I declare under the penalty of perjury that the above statement is true and correct to the best of my knowledge.

Date   Signature of Ronald Blackburn

                              Notary Seal and
                              Certification Here

Chapter 7 Highlights

Knowing what the VA will require in the way of evidence is an absolute must if you expect to submit a winning claim. You cannot protect your interest in the decisionmaking process if you do not know what the regulations dictate. You cannot win if you are unable to submit a well-grounded claim that is supported by evidence. You cannot win if you do not know how to collect this evidence. You cannot win if you do not know why the VA denies valid claims. You cannot win if you assume the VA is an all-knowing agency and that you can rely upon its skills to adjudicate the facts of the case accurately and fairly.

What do the regulations say about your claim before benefits can be granted? To answer that question you need to obtain a copy of pertinent sections of 38 CFR Parts 3 and 4. The CFR is available online and in local law libraries, VARO reading rooms, and university libraries designated as federal depositories.

Always keep in mind you have the burden of submitting a well-grounded claim. Equally important is your responsibility to satisfy the four basic elements of a claim for compensation benefits.

First, you must prove you were in the service. Second, you must demonstrate that an injury or illness did in fact occur while on active duty. Third, if the claim is not filed within one year after leaving the service or the medical condition is not universally accepted as being a medically chronic condition, evidence must be introduced of treatment that satisfies the continuity of symptomatology rule. Fourth, the medical condition that you are claiming as service related must be active when the claim is filed. Failing to satisfy each of these elements before submitting your claim will result in a denial of benefits.

Proof of Service: The VA requires an original Report of Separation (DD-214) or the equivalent. Its regulations allow for the acceptance of a certified copy from the clerk of the court where the original document was recorded. Do not send the VA an original discharge record. Always send a certified copy. If you have lost your original Report of Separation, a certified copy can be obtained from the NPRC.

Proof of Service Occurrence: Where do you look for this evidence? Start by requesting copies of all your outpatient and personnel records from the NPRC. Remember that inpatient hospital records are not stored with your personnel records. If you were hospitalized, submit a separate request for these documents providing specific information as to the hospital name and location, period of hospitalization, and reason for hospitalization.

Evidence of Treatment: When primary evidence cannot be located, you must then focus on building a claim based on secondary evidence. Copies of unit historical records often provide details of unit casualties that can substantiate a combat-related injury. Unit morning reports or PDCs will provide duty status for any given day. If you were hospitalized, the records will show the period of hospitalization but not why you were hospitalized. Official line of duty investigation is an excellent source for substantiating an injury.

If you were one of the service personnel used as a human guinea pig for the purpose of determining effects of biological agents, exposure to radiation, or various types of mind-controlling drugs, you can request records from government agencies under the provisions of the Freedom of Information Act. Probably thousands of individuals never realized they were unwilling participants in these tests. If you were one of them and you can prove it, you could be entitled to compensation benefits for the health problems created by the tests.

The VA must accept and treat sworn statements as it would any other form of evidence. A sworn statement from a former comrade is an excellent form of secondary evidence. The statement should reflect only observations, not unsubstantiated opinions. Your friend cannot give a medical opinion because he is not a physician. However, he can describe the observable symptoms and how they were affecting you.

As the claimant, you should always give a sworn statement. Detail all the events leading up to the injury or illness, how the illness has affected you, and what you cannot do now that you could do before you became disabled. A sworn statement should be straightforward and follow the examples above. Your goal is to get pertinent information into the record that would not normally be included.

Locating Witnesses: There are many ways of tracking down someone who might be able to give favorable testimony. Certain agencies of the United States government can forward a letter on your behalf. Internet telephone directories with their two hundred million listings are also an excellent tool in locating a former friend. Other techniques include classifieds in newspapers and monthly magazines of various veterans service organizations.

8 | FILING YOUR CLAIM

The Final Step: Make It Count

You are now ready to file a claim for a service-related disability, ask for an increase in benefits, amend a claim to include additional service disabilities, reopen a previously denied claim, or claim that your medical condition is considerably worse following treatment by a VA medical staff member. Once you've completed the appropriate form for the type of claim being filed, the next step is to organize all the evidence pertinent to the claim in a logical sequence.

Try to think of this process as if you were the adjudicator. In what order would you look at all the supporting documents and evidence to decide the merits of the claim? Remember these people cannot and will not spend hours looking through all the evidence, including military personnel and medical records, to search for confirmation of the facts that are alleged. As I have stated many times throughout this book, your claim will more than likely be reviewed by one individual who has only basic skills in medicine and law. The adjudication process is further complicated by the fact that the person deciding the claim will not have his decision reviewed in detail. If the adjudicator ignores favorable evidence, for whatever reason, no one will perform an in-depth review prior to the decision being finalized to determine if all the facts were considered and properly interpreted.

It has been my experience that what the adjudicators do not

understand, they ignore. They then deny the claim based solely on their own unsubstantiated conclusions. What they don't know, they deny. The message they are sending out is, "If you don't like it, take it up with the BVA. You will get a decision in two or three years." In the meantime they are easing the backlog of cases.

The organization of your claim must tell the whole story from beginning to end. When you have all this evidence, what do you do with it? Stuff it all in an envelope and send it to the regional office? No! Don't jeopardize all the effort put forth during the development phase by doing this.

You need to stay in control by forcing the VA to focus, in a logical manner, only on the facts supported by the evidence. Do not give the VA the latitude of deciding what is relevant. Prove that the claim is valid when it is submitted. Make the VA prove that the evidence is not valid and justify the denial of benefits. Always submit a claim knowing that it is grantable, and if it is denied at the local regional office level, it will be reversed on appeal. However, your real goal is to present the case so the adjudicator will be able to connect dots of evidence, like a child connecting dots to draw a picture. You want the benefits granted now, not in five years.

Organizing the Claim

Let me explain what I mean by organizing your claim. You want your evidence to tell a story and you want the adjudicator to follow it to only one conclusion: benefits approved. Sometimes this is easier said than done. The assembly process should allow the evidence to flow in one direction only, proving your entitlement to benefits.

To demonstrate the assembly process, I'll use the following

example. A veteran submitted an original claim in 2002 for service connection based on two medical conditions alleged to be service related. One condition is lung cancer and the second condition is due to a back injury.

The veteran served in the Air Force from 1969 to 1973 and was honorably discharged. The active duty outpatient health records show the veteran was treated for neck pain resulting from a whiplash injury when the jeep he was traveling in rear-ended another vehicle. The LOD of the accident stated that the veteran was a passenger in the jeep and was not at fault for the accident. It also showed that he was taken to the base hospital emergency department for treatment. He was admitted to the base hospital for three days, and the discharge diagnosis was severe cervical sprain resulting from whiplash. The service health records were silent as to any symptoms normally associated with lung cancer. The veteran is not a smoker and, following his discharge, worked in an office as a claims adjuster for an insurance company. The veteran suffered no physical injuries following his discharge.

The veteran was married twice after leaving the service. His first marriage was in 1977 and ended in a divorce two years later. In 1980 he remarried and two children were born of this union. His son was born in 1983 and the daughter was born in 1987. The veteran was never assigned a Permanent Change of Station to Vietnam. However, he was placed on temporary duty (TDY) on three occasions for a total of twelve weeks during his enlistment. As a photo intelligence interpreter he was assigned to Da Nang AFB, Cam Ranh Bay AFB, and Nha Trang AFB to support three special military intelligence operations. This is everything we know about the veteran.

A table of exhibits should be the first appended enclosure following the formal claim application. This table is very impor-

TABLE OF EXHIBITS

Exhibit Number	Description of Document	Number of Pages
Basic Documents		
E-1	Report of Separation DD-214	1
E-2	Copy of Marriage Licenses—Veteran	2
E-3	Copy of Divorce Decree—Veteran	1
E-4	Copy of Divorce & Marriage Certificates of Spouse [if applicable]	4
E-5	Copy of Children's Birth Certificates	2
E-6	Proof of Retired Pay [if applicable]	1
E-7	Proof of Disability or Downsizing Pay [if applicable]	1
Documents Supporting Disability #1—Neck injury		
E-8	Statement in Support of Claim	1
E-9	Copy of LOD by Captain Robert Jones	5
E-10	Copy of Base Hospital Inpatient Records	20
E-11	Copy of Outpatient Records—Neck Injury Treatment	35
E-12	Sworn Statements (Lay Evidence)	18
E-13	Copies of Postservice Medical Treatment Records	52
E-14	Medical Assessment of Dr. Robinson, Orthopedic Specialist	3
Documents Supporting Disability #2—Lung Cancer		
E-15	Statement in Support of Claim	2
E-16	Copy of TDY Orders Confirming Duty in Vietnam	3
E-17	Copy of Outpatient Treatment Records for Lung Cancer	85
E-18	Medical Assessment by Dr. Spencer, Cancer Specialist (Diagnosing Lung Cancer and Confirming Relationship to Agent Orange)	8

tant because it outlines the evidence and sequence of events pertinent to your claim. The format is quite simple.[1]

A statement in Support of Claim (E-8 and E-15) tells the VA why and what is being claimed. There is no specific format. It should be brief and to the point and typed. It is best if the statement is made using VA Form 21-4138.

In our hypothetical claim, the veteran injured his neck in a jeep accident. The accident happened in 1972, a year before he was discharged, and the claim was not filed until 1998, twenty-five years after he left the Air Force. The veteran needs to protect himself against a premature VA conclusion that the active duty injury resulted in no permanent disability and that the cause of the current problem occurred after leaving the service.

Because of the twenty-six-year lapse between the time of the injury and the filing of the claim, the veteran must show continuity of treatment. The veteran's statement focuses VA attention on the evidence concerning this injury·

> In 1972 I was a passenger in a jeep that rear-ended another army vehicle. I was hospitalized at McCord AFB for three days and was under outpatient care until my discharge. Following my release from the hospital, I was given a permanent physical profile change restricting my duties to administrative tasks only. I have been treated for chronic pain and limited motion of my neck for nearly twenty-five years.

---

[1] Each exhibit number should be prominently displayed on the lower left corner of each page. If there is more than one page for the exhibit, identification should be expressed in this format: E-10, page 5 of 35. It is very important to place your social security number in the lower right corner of every page.

My wife of eighteen years has provided a sworn affidavit that during our marriage I was never injured or in an accident that would cause the medical problems I have endured. I am no longer able to work because of this injury and my lung cancer. My orthopedic specialist states that the neck injury is old and that the type of accident I was involved in is typical of the type of cervical spine problems currently diagnosed.

The Statement in Support of Claim concerning lung cancer should address several points concerning lung cancer resulting from exposure to Agent Orange. This is one of the disabilities that are presumed to be service related if it has manifested to a degree of 10 percent disabling within thirty years from date of exposure. Here again the statement should be brief and to the point.

Between 1970 and 1972 I was placed on TDY status to the Republic of Vietnam to support special military exercise for a total of three months. I file this claim under the provisions of 38 CFR §3.309(e) as amended on May 8, 2001, for presumptive service connection for respiratory cancer. My evidence includes copies of orders that placed me TDY in Vietnam and my oncologist's medical assessment stating that I am currently being treated for lung cancer.

Assembly Process

By preparing a table of exhibits, you present your case in an orderly manner and force the VA to focus only on the key issues involved. You minimize the danger that vital evidence will be overlooked. Arrange the evidence by date, starting with the earliest record and advancing to the most recent record. This is especially important when medical treatment records are a major part of the evidentiary package. If you are claiming more than one disability, this sequence should be repeated for each disability being claimed.

With medical records, review each page and highlight those sections that specifically support your claim. Look for and highlight every relevant diagnosis you find in your records. One reason this step is important is that it can establish chronicity or continuity of treatment. Remove from the copies of medical records any treatment records that are not directly related to the conditions being claimed. You do not want to provide them with any information other than what will support your claim.

Submitting the Claim

Before you submit the claim application, look over all VA forms making certain only those items applicable to your claim are answered. If VA Form 21-4138, Statement in Support of Claim, is handwritten, make certain it is readable. When completing a formal application, remember to write "N/A" for all those item numbers and sections not requiring a written response. Answer all required questions accurately and completely.

With this task completed, have your entire application photocopied. You will always need to back up any information you provide the VA. If you are able to hand-deliver the application to the regional office, do so. Have the Contact Office representative who accepts your claim application package date-stamp your copy of each document and form. Among the millions of documents and files circulated within the VA, records and evidence get lost every day. Without proof that you actually submitted a claim or submitted evidence, the burden is on you to prove you filed a well-grounded claim and that you submitted supporting evidence.

When a claim is unable to be delivered directly to the VARO, the only alternative is to send the application and all supporting evidence by certified mail with return receipt requested. Before taking your complete claim package to be copied, obtain and complete Postal Service Form 3811 (Domestic Return Receipt) and Postal Service Form 3800 (Receipt for Certified Mail). Write the number found on the Receipt for Certified Mail form on the upper right-hand corner of each page of your claim package. Record this number in box 4a on the Domestic Return Receipt form as well. Now have copies made of the entire package.

The Post Office will date-stamp Form 3800, affix the lower portion to the envelope with your claim, and give you the top portion with the date stamped on it. When the Domestic Return Receipt is returned, you will have a copy of the original PS Forms 3800 and 3811 dated and signed, a copy of your complete claim package with the certified mail number on each page, and the Receipt for Certified Mail date-stamped by the post office. You now have absolute proof that the VA accepted your claim package in its entirety. If a claim or any evidence is lost, the VA has the burden of proving that it did not lose your documents. This little procedure could save you thousands of dollars that might be lost if you cannot positively show when you submitted your claim.

The last step before mailing or hand-carrying your claim to the local regional office is to make sure the claim forms and all evidence will remain together. The VA secures all hardcopy forms and evidence in claim folders with a two-prong fastener located on the top of the file cover. Using a two-hole punch, centered, punch holes at the top of each form and document. Secure the claim with all its supporting evidence with a two-prong metal fastener. They can be purchased in any office supply store.

Chapter 8 Highlights

Although this is one of the shortest chapters in the book, it is by no means unimportant. Actually, how you put your claim together and the method used in filing the claim will have a direct bearing on the outcome. The VA is *not* user friendly and will not spend hours reviewing every document to ensure that you receive all benefits due. The law says it is supposed to, but don't count on it.

The VA is always looking for ways to disallow a claim based on it not being "well grounded." This is why you want to organize all your evidence and provide a table of exhibits so that you can lead the VA to a favorable decision. You cannot take shortcuts and hope the VA either won't notice a missing link of evidence or will sort through everything to grant benefits. Remember, the burden of proof is on you to prove the claim is well grounded.

The assembly of your claim and all its supporting evidence must follow a logical path. Each piece of evidence must link to the next and so on. For each disability claimed I suggest preparing a Statement in Support of Claim (VA Form 21-4138) as illustrated above. It's important that you tell the VA what you are claiming and even the authority under which the claim should be granted. By making the VA look specifically at that one authority, it must, if denying your claim, explain exactly why your contentions and evidence do not qualify.

Once you're ready to send in your claim, take the time to

properly identify every piece of paper that is attached to the claim. If you hand-deliver your claim to the regional office and the clerk will not date-stamp every page of your copy, *do not leave the claim.* Mail the claim and documentation by certified mail with return receipt requested, using the technique discussed in this chapter. It's no exaggeration that the VA loses documents, forms, statements, and evidence every day. Don't let it be yours.

What Makes a Well-Grounded Claim?

The first question you must ask is, "Is the evidence sufficient to convince a fair and impartial individual that the claim is plausible?" This is the key to establishing a well-grounded claim. If the claim is initially denied because it was considered not well grounded, the only recourse is to appeal that decision. However, the appeal can address only one issue: was evidence adequate to satisfy the initial burden of submitting a well-grounded claim? It will take two to three years before the issue is decided. If the claimant is successful on appeal, only then will the VA proceed with the task of determining whether the evidence is sufficient to grant service connection for disabilities claimed.

Problems Created by a Weakly Supported Claim

The concept of a well-grounded claim can best be understood by analyzing a typical claim action submitted twenty to thirty years after leaving the service. Our claimant was in the U.S. Air Force from 1962 to 1966 and stationed in Arizona. He was a crew chief assigned to one of the fighter's squadrons and performed all his duties outside on the flight line. In 1965, while home on leave, he was involved in an automobile accident that caused a cervical neck injury. He received an honorable discharge.

In January 1996 he filed an original claim for ankylosis of the cervical spine, alleging that the automobile accident in 1965 was the cause of his severe neck condition. He also filed a claim for basal cell carcinoma on the basis that he was continuously exposed to the sun for four years while working on the flight line. A detailed statement by the claimant of the accident and a copy of the police report were attached to the application as supporting evidence. However, the report was silent as to any injuries he may have suffered. To support his claim for skin cancer he stated he worked on aircraft outside on the flight line for four years. His former line chief submitted a buddy letter attesting to that fact. The claimant also attached a letter from his doctor stating that he was suffering from basal cell carcinoma. The VA denied the claim on the grounds it was not well grounded.

The local VARO's rationale for denying the claim was that the claimant did not submit medical evidence indicating his neck injury was caused by the 1965 automobile accident. The VA further contended that the medical evidence submitted to justify service connection for skin cancer did not prove his contention that the condition occurred while he was in the Air Force. The claimant's service records could not be found at the National Record Center; they may have been destroyed in the 1973 fire.

The decision was appealed and forwarded to the BVA, who affirmed the local regional office's decision. The BVA ruled that to establish service connection without the service records, medical experts would have to review postservice treatment and determine that the current conditions were linked to the service.

The claimant went back to the VA, trying to reopen his claim by providing dates, names, and addresses of those who could give evidence to substantiate his claim. Once again the regional office denied his request on the basis that he did not provide new and material evidence as required under 38 CFR §3.156. The decision was appealed and two years later, the BVA affirmed the regional office's denial of benefits.

The claimant appealed the BVA's decision to the United States Court of Appeals for Veterans Claims. More than a year passed before the court ruled that the claim was well grounded. The claimant's statement, the buddy statement, doctor's assessment, and traffic accident report were sufficient to determine the claim was well grounded. The case was remanded to the BVA with instruction to comply with the "duty to assist" provision of the law. Now more than five years later, the VA is going to determine if the claimant is entitled to service connected benefits for residuals of an automobile accident and skin cancer.

Defining "Well-Grounded Claim" by Case Law

Title 38 U.S. Code §5107(a) provides that "A person who submits a claim for benefits under a law administered by the Secretary shall have the burden of submitting evidence sufficient to justify a belief by a fair and impartial individual that the claim is well-grounded." What this means is, if a claim is submitted based only on a belief that the current medical condition was related to your military service without sufficient proof, it will be considered frivolous and denied. You cannot invoke the VA's duty to assist unless the claim is considered well grounded.

Fortunately, the United States Court of Appeals for Veterans Claims has provided considerable case law to assist in our understanding of a well-grounded claim. These decisions outline the claimant's responsibility before the VA is mandated to discharge its duty to assist. These same decisions tell the VA exactly what it can and cannot do before denying a claim as not well grounded.

Key Decisions from the United States Court of Appeals for Veterans Claims

The issue of a well-grounded claim has been before the Court of Appeals for Veterans Claims many times, and each time the definition is refined. One of the first decisions by the court was *Murphy v. Derwinski, 1 Vet. App. 78 (1990),* which said that "a well-grounded claim is one which is meritorious on its own or capable of substantiation. Such a claim need not be conclusive but only possible to satisfy the initial burden as stated in Title 38 United States Code §5107(a)." Even with this liberal interpretation by the court of a well-grounded claim, regional offices routinely deny claims. All a rating board member has to say is "I don't think the evidence is sufficient to be considered meritorious or substantial." Then for the next three to five years you have to hand-wrestle them over this one issue alone.

In *Tirpak v. Derwinski, 2 Vet. App. 609 (1992),* the court ruled that "to be well-grounded, a claim must be accompanied by supportive evidence and that such evidence must justify a belief by a fair and impartial individual that the claim is plausible." VA instructions to rating board members emphasized that entitlement to compensation benefits requires more than an allegation of entitlement to benefits. A claimant must submit supporting evidence. Evidence can consist of many diverse items such as VA or private medical records, service records, lay statements, or the veteran's own testimony.

In *Rabideau v. Derwinski, 2 Vet. App. 141 (1992),* the court established that there must be evidence of a current disability in order for a claim for service connection to be well grounded. Again, in *Brammer v. Derwinski, 3 Vet. App. 233 (1992)* the court revisited this issue of having an existing medical problem at the time the claim is filed:

> There is a more fundamental basis for affirmance (that is, confirmation) of the BVA in this case. In neither the claim concerning spinal meningitis nor the 'new' claim concerning frozen feet has the appellant produced any evidence, medical or otherwise, that would tend to show a presently existing disability stemming from either spinal meningitis or frozen feet.

In *Proscelle v. Derwinski, 2 Vet. App. 629 (1992)*, the court noted that in order to trigger the VA's duty to assist, the claimant must submit sufficient evidence to justify a belief by a fair and impartial individual that the claim is well grounded. In this case the claimant filed a claim for increased benefits for his service-connected condition. The VA denied his request for increased benefits on the basis it was not well grounded. However, the court held that the claim was plausible and capable of substantiation.

The next significant decision made by the court was *Grottveit v. Brown, 5 Vet. App. 91 (1993)*. The court stated that the quality and quantity of evidence required to meet the statutory burden for establishing a well-grounded claim depend upon the issue presented by the claim. Where the issue is factual in nature, competent lay testimony, including the veteran's solitary testimony, may constitute sufficient evidence to establish a well-grounded claim. A good example would be the automobile accident we used to illustrate a well-grounded claim. When an issue involves a medical cause or medical diagnosis, competent medical evidence is necessary to establish a well-grounded claim. Here again the example used at the beginning of this section demonstrates the importance of this decision.

The court, in deciding *King v. Brown, 5 Vet. App. 19 (1993)*, stated that the truthfulness of evidence is presumed in determining whether a claim is well grounded and that if the claimant makes evidentiary statements on or accompanying a VA Form 21-526, those statements must be accepted as true for the purpose of determining whether the claim is well grounded.

The court further refined the meaning of "well-grounded" when deciding *Lathan v. Brown, 7 Vet. App. 359 (1995)*. It affirmed that the threshold of plausibility to make a well-grounded claim is considerably lower than the threshold for new and material evidence to justify reopening a claim. Referring to *Tirpak,* the court stated that "Medicine is more art than exact science, nor . . . does it [the Tirpak decision] stand for the proposition that a medical opinion must be expressed in terms of certainty in order to serve as the basis for a well-grounded claim."

Another action by the court on the subject of a well-grounded claim was *Robinette v. Brown, 8 Vet. App. 69 (1995)*. The court noted that the VA adjudication process is nonadversarial. The well-grounded claim requirement applicable in that process parallels the rule applied in civil actions that facts alleged are accepted as true for the purpose of determining if relief can be granted. When a claim is adjudicated, both the weight and credibility of the evidence must be determined as a question of fact. The court's jurisprudence makes clear that

to be well-grounded a claim need not be supported by evidence sufficient for the claim to be granted. Rather the law establishes only a preliminary threshold of plausibility with enough of an evidentiary basis to show that the claim is capable of substantiation. A vital element of substantiation of a well-grounded claim is the execution of the Secretary's duty to assist a claimant.

Morton v. West, 12 Vet. App. 447, 486 (1999) is an extremely important decision because it actually touches on two doctrines: the veteran's duty to submit a well-grounded claim and the VA's duty to assist. The court affirmed in this case that the VA has no authority to issue regulations inconsistent with the statutory requirement that would justify a belief by a fair and impartial individual that the claim is well grounded before the VA is required to assist in developing the claims.

This decision invalidated any VA directives or procedures which pertain to volunteer VA assistance in all claims, even if they are not well grounded, by holding that such directives or procedures are inconsistent with 38 U.S.C. §5107(a). The veteran in this case initially appealed his denial of benefits because the VA failed to assist him in developing his claim as outlined in the M21-1 adjudication manual. However, the court pointed out in its decision that these instructions were contrary to the statute.

Reeling from the impact of this decision, the American Legion, on behalf of all veterans, filed a suit against the VA in the United States Court of Appeals for the Federal Circuit, Washington, DC. In 2001, Congress passed a law that made the court's decision in *Morton v. West* moot. The VA is now required by law to assist the veteran in developing their claim before deciding whether the claim is well grounded.

Chapter 9 Highlights

Each regional office must follow a set of guidelines when considering whether a claim is well grounded. If the claim is denied, the VARO must follow the correct procedures for denying the claim.

For a claim to trigger the VA's duty to assist, the claimant is responsible for the following:

- For a disabling condition, the veteran must attach medical proof which demonstrates he is currently suffering from the alleged condition and it is possibly related to the service.
- When the claim is reviewed, the accumulative evidence of record must support the claim and the last VA medical examination must affirm the existence of the condition.
- If a statement of a medical causation or relationship is made by a layperson, a medical authority must confirm it. For example, using a buddy letter contending skin cancer was caused by working out in the sun for four years is acceptable as long as a doctor's diagnosis confirms skin cancer and that such exposure could have caused the skin cancer.
- If a medical treatise was used suggesting service connection, it must be accompanied by medical evidence from a doctor that the information was relevant to the case.
- If the claim is for multiple disabilities, the evidence for each individual disability must be able to stand alone before triggering the VA's duty to assist for that medical condition.

When the rating or authorization activity decides that the claim is not well grounded, the notification to the claimant must clearly explain why the claim is considered an incomplete application and why the regional office is not taking further action. In addition, the notification must advise the claimant what evidence is necessary to make the claim well-grounded.

The letter of denial will also tell the claimant he has one year from the date of notification to submit the required evidence. If the evidence submitted is sufficient to justify the standard of being a well-grounded claim, the effective date of any benefits awarded will be the date of the original claim.

10 | THE VA'S DUTY TO ASSIST

Background

The claimant's understanding of the VA's duty to assist is as important to the success of the claim action as submitting a well-grounded claim. Knowing what the VA must do and what it will not do is essential. In preparing a claim you cannot assume the evidence is sufficient or that the VA will develop all relevant facts before the issue is decided. You must know exactly what is involved in the adjudication process before the rating board is permitted to decide the case. The Department of Veterans Affairs published a summary of significant holdings by the United States Court of Appeals for Veterans Claims for the benefit of all adjudication personnel. This case law has had significant impact on the adjudication of claims for veterans benefits. By the end of 1995, the Veterans Benefits Administration had reviewed more than 7,500 court decisions and prepared nearly seven hundred decision assessment documents. The results of this effort have brought about recommendations for more than one hundred changes to VA regulations, policies, or procedures. Yet despite all this guidance, we see very little change in the number of claims being granted without being forced into the appeal process.

What the VA Must Do to Satisfy Its Duty to Assist

Although the VA has a statutory obligation to assist a claimant in developing facts pertinent to a well-grounded claim (38

U.S.C. §5107(a)), a limited duty exists even when a claim is not well grounded. The denial letter must inform the claimant what evidence is required to make the claim well grounded. The claimant then has one year to get this evidence and submit it to the VA. If the denial letter does not clearly indicate what evidence is needed to establish a well-grounded claim, file a Notice of Disagreement citing *Robinette v. Brown, 8 Vet. App. 69 (1995)*. The notice to the VA can be quite simple: "Your letter of denial has failed to comply with the precedent-setting ruling of the court in *Robinette v. Brown, 8 Vet. App. 69 (1995)*. I was not advised exactly what evidence was required in order to satisfy the requirements of a well-grounded claim."

By law, the VA's duty to assist includes requesting any information from other federal departments or agencies that may be needed to determine eligibility and entitlement or to verify evidence (38 U.S.C. §5106). Federal regulation 38 CFR §3.159 requires adjudication personnel to request other records such as hospital reports or copies of doctor's records when a release is provided.

Case Law: Defining "Duty to Assist"

"Duty to assist" obligations generally involve development of all relevant facts from all identified sources, both government and civilian (including lay evidence). The VA must request all historical medical records in service-connected disability claims. In addition, Social Security Administration (SSA) records must be obtained to consider claims for increase, individual unemployability, and disability pension. The VA is also obliged to obtain and consider SSA records when there is evidence that they may be relevant to a finding of service connection. The court found in *Lind v. Principi, 3 Vet. App.*

493 (1992) that the VA should have developed SSA records to consider presumptive service connection for multiple sclerosis because there was a possibility that the documents might show onset of the disease within the presumptive period.

In fulfilling its duty to assist, the court ruled in *Douglas v. Derwinski, 2 Vet. App. 435 (1992)* that the VA must consider all issues, which may be inferred from a liberal reading of an appeal and the evidence. An issue may not be ignored or rejected merely because the veteran did not expressly raise the appropriate legal provision for the benefit sought. In *Douglas v. Derwinski* the court concluded that evidence implicating military sun exposure as a cause of basal cell carcinoma raised a well-grounded claim for direct service connection even though the appellant's contention focused on ionizing radiation instead.

When the claimant references or describes specific private medical records, VA medical records, or other records, which he believes may be relevant, the duty to assist requires the VA to attempt to obtain the referenced records without prejudging their relevance. A good example would be obtaining vocational rehabilitation counseling and evaluation records because they may contain relevant information regarding the degree of employability.

If a veteran tries to reopen a denied claim, the VA must develop the facts pertinent to the issue being sought, even though the evidence may ultimately prove insufficient to reopen the claim when it is finally decided. The court ruled in *Ivey v. Derwinski, 2 Vet. App. 320 (1992)* that complete development is required if there is some legal or factual basis for potential allowance.

The duty to assist is heightened when there is no opportunity for personal contact (such as in the case of incarcerated veterans) or when complete service medical records are not available (such as with POW records or the service records destroyed by the 1973 fire at the NPRC). This diligent effort to obtain records is required when the records are in control of a government agency or when only official copies of records from government sources would be reliable or relevant. This special effort must also be made when searching for records associated with disabilities incurred or aggravated in combat.

The affirmative duty of the VA to assist is also triggered when a veteran appears before a local VA hearing officer. These officers *must* explain the issues to the veteran and suggest what evidence is needed to support the claim. A hearing officer is required to request all evidence that is alleged to exist that might support the veteran's claim. The court held in *Weggenmann v. Brown, 5 Vet. App. 281 (1993)* that while VA regulations provide that a claimant may request a physical examination during a hearing, an official reexamination is required only if the prior examination was inadequate.

There is a duty to assist any time a potential claim for possible benefits exists. The VA is obligated to inform the claimants about the application requirements for unclaimed benefits if there is a potential claim. An example would be if during a records review the VA discovered the veteran suffered a serious acoustic trauma while in the service. The potential for establishing a service-connected hearing loss is possible; therefore, the VA must inform the individual of the right to file for this disability.

In *Connolly v. Derwinski, 1 Vet. App. 566 (1991),* the duty to assist was further clarified. The court held the VA must respond to a specific request for assistance by initiating appropriate development or by explaining why the requested assistance has been denied. If a veteran does not wish to undergo further VA examination, the VA must explain the importance of the examination that was ordered so that the veteran may make an informed decision.

The VA has often failed in its duty to assist claimants when it requests the veteran be scheduled for a C&P Examination at a VA hospital or clinic. In *Hayes v. Brown, 5 Vet. App. 60 (1993)*, the court held that the duty to assist is not met when a prescribed duty is overlooked, such as if a VA physician fails to render a required medical opinion or the VA fails to develop pertinent medical evidence despite a specific request. More generally, the VA's access to necessary information, efforts to obtain relevant information, and the claimant's cooperation are all factors for determining whether or not the VA has fulfilled its obligations in a particular case.

VA medical examinations have been mandated by the court based on duty-to-assist considerations when

- there is evidence of a significant change in a veteran's condition affecting pension entitlement.
- a thorough and contemporaneous examination, including review of prior medical treatment records, may resolve diagnostic questions pertinent to service connection.
- medical records are received after an examination that may have been pertinent to the examiner's findings.
- an opinion concerning possible medical relationships between past and present disorders may be relevant to a finding of service connection or there is a question as to the cause of increased disability during active duty.
- verification of current disability is necessary in order to establish service connection.

- increased disability is claimed and the record does not adequately show the current level of impairment due to service-connected disability.
- a prior VA examination was inadequate.
- a VA examiner recommends supplemental or specialist examinations.
- a plausible claim for service connection is filed within an applicable presumptive period even though a prior claim during that period for the same condition was finally denied.
- in a service-connected death case, an advisory medical opinion is required, in lieu of VA examination, when necessary to resolve medical questions pertinent to service connection.

The VA Duty to Assist Is Limited

The duty to assist is not unlimited. The VA has no duty to assist unqualified applicants or develop inherently incredible (not well-grounded) allegations. The extent of VA assistance may be limited if the claimant fails to notify the VA of all relevant records or fails to cooperate with the VA during the development process.

In *Owings v. Brown, 8 Vet. App. 17 (1995)*, the court held in regards to notification requirements that the VA is not required to notify former recipients of DIC benefits who lost their status as surviving spouse of changes in the law regarding DIC benefits. Along with that, a similar 1994 decision, *Harvey v. Brown, 6 Vet. App. 416 (1994)*, affirmed that the VA's duty to assist does not include an obligation, prior to discharge from active duty, to assist in preparing a claim for certain education benefits that the veteran indicated to the VA that he wanted to take.

The duty of the VA to search for documents is limited to those that have been specifically identified and which by their description would be relevant and material to the claim. The VA has stated that its policy is to consider the merits of each claim as fully and as expeditiously as possible. However, all adjudication personnel have been advised that because of the potential **probative** value of a record it should not be prejudged.

The duty to assist ends when all relevant evidence is obtained, or cannot be obtained despite reasonable efforts, or when benefits are granted. While the VA must consider evidence that can confirm entitlement, there is no duty-to-assist requirement to develop additional records when entitlement can be established on the evidence of record.

Chapter 10 Highlights

The court has issued numerous decisions regarding the VA's duty to assist. Not only have these decisions been very specific with respect to defining "duty to assist," but they also were interpreted very liberally to benefit the claimant. It's important to remember these points any time a claim action is filed:

- A claim must be well grounded before the VA has a duty to assist.
- If the claim is denied on the basis of not being well grounded, the VA must indicate what evidence is needed to qualify the claim. The claim remains open for one year from the date of notification.
- The VA policy since December 1993 requires the regional office, when notifying a claimant that the claim is not well grounded, to clearly explain why the specific issue(s) raised

is(are) not considered well-grounded and why further action on the claim is not being taken at this time.

- If another federal department or agency has evidence that
is pertinent to the claim, the VA is required by law to
contact this source and retrieve this information if it has
been duly notified of its existence.
- "Duty to assist" means the VA must develop all relevant
facts from all identified sources, both government and
civilian, including lay evidence.
- The VA must request all historical medical records in
service-connected disability claims.
- Social security records *must* be developed when considering claims for increased benefits, individual unemployability, and disability pension, or when the claimant is receiving social security benefits for the same disability for which
VA benefits are being claimed.
- The VA may not ignore or reject a claim merely because
the veteran did not correctly raise the appropriate legal
provision for the benefit sought.
- The VA must completely develop a claim if there is some
legal or factual basis for possible benefits.
- When searching for records related to disabilities incurred
or aggravated in combat, the VA must make a special
effort.
- If the VA loses the records, the claimant is a POW, or
the fire at the NRC destroyed the records, the duty to assist
is heightened.
- If the claimant appears before a VA hearing officer, the
duty to assist is triggered, requiring the hearing officer to
explain the issues and suggest the evidence necessary to
support the claim.
- The VA must respond to a specific request for assistance by

initiating appropriate development or explaining in writing why the request is being denied.

- The duty to assist is not met if the VA overlooks a prescribed duty, such as, for example, accepting a VA medical examination when the doctor did not comply with the *Physician's Guide for Disability Evaluation Examinations*.

11 DOCTRINE OF REASONABLE DOUBT

Concept of the Doctrine of Reasonable Doubt

The last statement added to every rating decision by the rating board is a certification that the Doctrine of Reasonable Doubt was considered in deciding the issues of the claim. This is without doubt one of the most important concepts written into the law governing veterans benefits. Failure by a rating board to correctly apply this provision of the law when rating a claim is grounds for remand or reversal on appeal. A claimant or advocate needs to understand this concept to ensure that benefits justified are benefits granted.

The most common statement I've seen on rating decisions denying entitlement is "Granting of the benefits sought due to reasonable doubt under 38 CFR §3.102 was considered but the rating board concluded that the *fair preponderance of evidence* [emphasis added] was not in the veteran's favor and the rule had no application." Yet this statement as written is not in compliance with the guidance and definition provided by the court in *Gilbert v. Derwinski, 1 Vet. App. 49 (1990)*.

The court stated,

> When, after consideration of all evidence and material of record, in cases before the Department of Veterans Affairs, there is an approximate balance of positive and negative evidence regarding the merits of an issue material to the determination of the matter, the benefit of doubt in resolving each such issue shall be given to the

claimant. . . . Therefore, a veteran need only demonstrate that there is an 'approximate balance of positive and negative evidence' in order to prevail; entitlement need not be established beyond a reasonable doubt, or by clear and convincing evidence, or by a reasonable doubt, or by a fair preponderance of evidence.

The court further stated that the secretary agreed at oral arguments that the preponderance of the evidence must be against the claim for benefits to be denied.

It's obvious that the rating board did not grasp this concept when they rated the claim from which I gave the quote. The VA has to show a preponderance of evidence against the claim. The guidance from the court in *Gilbert v. Derwinski* provided a definition for "approximate balance of positive and negative evidence." Simply, the phrase means evidence that does not satisfactorily prove or disprove the claim; there is one other requirement for a rating board when they deny a claim. They must explain exactly what evidence tipped the scales against the claim. They cannot simply say, "Granting of the benefits sought due to reasonable doubt under 38 CFR §3.102 was considered, but the rating board concluded that the fair preponderance of the evidence was not in the veteran's favor and the rule had no application" or words to that effect. If your claim is denied and the only reference to the Doctrine of Reasonable Doubt is some vague statement, appeal the denial. The law requires the VA to give detailed reasons and bases for any action it takes.

Case Law: Defining the Concept of Reasonable Doubt

The issue of whether the VA has considered the Doctrine of Reasonable Doubt has been before the United States Court of

Appeals for Veterans Claims on numerous occasions. By the same token, the BVA has remanded or reversed local regional offices seventy-eight times during 1994 and 1995 on this very issue. Regional offices have considerable difficulty grasping this concept. It would be an understatement to say that if every veteran were knowledgeable of this doctrine when the claim was submitted and decided, the VA would be overwhelmed with appeals. A veteran who files a well-documented claim needs to know what the VA must prove by way of negative evidence before it can deny the application for benefits.

GILBERT V. DERWINSKI, 1 VET. APP. 49 (1990)

The Gilbert decision was a landmark case decided by the court because it considered three statutory provisions of the law. The court addressed the following issues: when it could set aside a BVA finding of material fact as clearly erroneous; the intent of giving the veteran the benefit of the doubt as written into the law; and whether the VA was in compliance with the statute when it failed to provide a written statement of the reasons or bases for its factual findings and conclusions of law.

Mr. Gilbert filed a claim for service connection alleging an in-service back injury of which he was currently suffering the residuals. The BVA upheld the denial of his claim, finding that he had not demonstrated that any back injury occurred during military service and that even if such an injury did occur it was "apparently acute and transitory in nature and resolved without leaving any residual disability." The BVA then concluded that in view of this finding he was not entitled to the benefit of the doubt.

On review the court found that the BVA decision did not include an analysis of the credibility or probative value of the evidence submitted by and on behalf of the veteran in support of the claim. The BVA failed to provide any explanation for the bare conclusion that "the Board [BVA] does not find that [the] doctrine [of reasonable doubt] would warrant allowance of the benefit sought on appeal." The court concluded that the decision failed to comply with 38 U.S.C. §4004(d)(1) (1988) (now §7104(d)(2)), which requires that a written statement of reasons or bases for its factual findings and conclusions of law be provided to the veteran. Thus the court remanded the case to the BVA with instruction to comply with the law.

WILLIS V. DERWINSKI, 1 VET. APP. 63 (1990)

The Willis case is another example of the VA saying that although it considered the Doctrine of Reasonable Doubt there was no evidence in which to grant benefits under the doctrine. In actuality, the BVA ignored the principles of the doctrine by failing to provide reasons or bases for its conclusion that the veteran was not entitled to the benefits of the doctrine.

Mr. Willis filed a claim to establish schizophrenia as a service connection disability based on the argument that his nervous condition was misdiagnosed on active duty. Six months after filing his claim Mr. Willis was examined by the VA and found to be suffering from chronic paranoid schizophrenia. He was reexamined six months later and the medical diagnosis was the same. Fifteen months after he filed his original claim, the VA notified him that his claim file, VA examinations, and service medical records were lost and could not be located. Three months later he received a letter of denial stating that his claim for a nervous condition was previously denied ten years earlier. The letter went on to say, "It must be assumed that service connection for a nervous condition was disallowed in 1979 and that you were informed of this decision."

When the case finally made its way to the United States Court of Appeals for Veterans Claims, it was remanded to the BVA. The court noted,

> Given the loss of the veteran's service medical records [the "contemporaneous medical record"] and his claims file by the VA, this statement [VA doctor's report] serves only to state the obvious; it does not refute the evidence in favor of the claim. . . . His [the VA doctor's] conclusion that the veteran's psychosis was misdiagnosed by the Air Force as a personality disorder, if not refuted, would appear to establish the veteran's claim.

In its remand order the court ruled that the VA failed to articulate "reasons or bases" for the apparent dismissal of evidence of record favorable to the veteran and the "reasons or basis" for its conclusion that the veteran was not entitled to the benefit of the doubt under 38 U.S.C. §5107(b).

O'HARE V. DERWINSKI, 1 VET. APP. 365 (1991)

The O'Hare decision is an example of an original claim denied by the local regional office and affirmed by the BVA that involved records destroyed in the 1973 fire at the NPRC. Mr. O'Hare filed a claim for chronic right knee disability that he alleges happened in the service. The injury occurred during a hike in the snow at Ft. Sheridan between November 1944 and February 1945. Mr. O'Hare maintains that he sought medical care for this injury at the base hospital and that he has been treated for this impairment throughout the past forty-five years. In support of his claim, the veteran submitted letters from his private physician and his two sisters. His doctor stated that "persistent problems with pain in the right hip and knee . . .

required local physical therapy, anti-inflammatories and joint injections . . . [and bother the appellant] on a fairly regular basis." His sisters stated that "when the veteran went into the army . . . he had no leg problems and when he came out . . . he had hurt his leg and thigh, . . . went to doctors the last forty-five years [and] takes pain pills."

The court held that the BVA decision did not meet the instruction of 38 U.S.C. §4004(d)(1) (1988) [now 38 U.S.C. §7104(d)(1) (1992)] in that the BVA's findings and conclusions are not accompanied by

> reasons or bases adequate to explain both to the veteran and the court its factual findings and its conclusions, [including] identifying those findings it deems crucial to its decision and accounting for the evidence which it finds to be persuasive or unpersuasive. . . . The BVA decision here fails to meet this prescription in two important respects.
>
> First, the decision fails to include an analysis of the credibility or probative value of the evidence submitted by or on behalf of the veteran in support of his claim. . . . The Board (BVA) made no express credibility determinations regarding the statements of either the veteran or his sister, or the letter from his physician. Such determinations are required.
>
> [Second, the] reason or basis requirement of 38 U.S.C. §4004(d)(1) [now §7104(d)(1)] applies to the Board's [BVA] conclusion that the veteran is not entitled to the "benefit of doubt" under 38 U.S.C. §3007(b) [now §5107(b)]. Here the BVA decision treats the benefit-of-the-doubt standard in only the most conclusory terms. . . . The doctrine of reasonable doubt has been consid-

ered, but the evidence is not found to be so evenly balanced as to warrant allowance of the claim. *That is not enough* [emphasis added].

This [the Doctrine of Reasonable Doubt] is especially so [significant] in a case where the service medical records are presumed destroyed; in such a case, the BVA's obligation to explain its findings and conclusions and to consider carefully the benefit-of-the-doubt rule is heightened.

FLUHARTY V. DERWINSKI 2 VET. APP. 409 (1992)

In Fluharty's case, the VA failed to consider the Doctrine of Reasonable Doubt as it applies to a reopened claim for a total disability rating due to individual unemployability. Mr. Fluharty served eighteen months in the U.S. Army before he was given a medical discharge for a fractured right ankle in 1963. During his enlistment he injured his lower back and right thumb. The VA initially granted the veteran a 40 percent rating for the residual of his injured right ankle and 0 percent for his fractured thumb. In 1980, service connection for his lower back injury was granted and rated 20 percent disabling. A claim for individual unemployability was filed in 1980 and subsequently denied.

Mr. Fluharty applied for increased benefits because of the severity of his back condition and was awarded 40 percent in 1985. Two years later the VA granted service connection for a right knee condition and rated it 10 percent disabling and gave a zero percent rating for sexual impotence due to a loss of a creative organ. He now had a combined disability rating of 70 percent.

In 1988, the veteran filed an action to reopen his claim for total disability due to individual unemployability and for an increased rating for all service-connected disabilities. Mr. Fluharty had not worked since his medical discharge in 1963. When his claim for increased benefits was denied in late 1988, the veteran filed a Notice of Disagreement and initiated the appeal process. He was called in for two VA examinations while his appeal was under consideration.

The orthopedic physician diagnosed a fractured right ankle with fibrotic ankylosis and severe arthritis of the right ankle. This report also pointed out that the "Patient is unable to work. . . . He has a stiff right ankle and it is a severe disability. . . . He will not improve in the future. . . . He is not employable. There is no treatment that would improve his condition. . . . [I] recommend that the patient have a total disability." The other VA examiner stated the appellant's unemployability was a combination of both his service-connected and non-service-connected disabilities. His report stated, "This patient has multiple medical problems along with low pack pain and right leg pain. He also suffers from significant depression. He has angina and uses six to eight nitroglycerine tablets every week. When I see him at the office, he has a hard time walking from the waiting room to my examining room. He is unable to get on and off the examining table. I consider him totally disabled."

The BVA upheld the local regional office denial of benefits in April 1990. The veteran filed a timely appeal to the United States Court of Appeals for Veterans Claims.

The case was decided two years later on May 18, 1992, by a three-judge panel. The court vacated the denial of benefits based on individual unemployability and remanded the case to the BVA. The court made these points when it sided with the veteran:

- Total disability rating "will be considered to exist when there is present any impairment of mind or body which is sufficient to render it impossible for the average person to follow a substantially gainful occupation."
- The appellant has a combined disability rating of 70 percent from December 17, 1985, plus special monthly compensation under 38 U.S.C. §1114(k), for the loss of a creative organ.
- The BVA voiced an opinion that the appellant cannot do "physically demanding" work, supporting its previous finding that he was capable of performing sedentary employment such as "light manual labor." Although the BVA has voiced an opinion as to whether the appellant is employable, it has not provided reasons or bases in support of its finding that the appellant is employable. The records show the appellant appears periodically in a wheelchair.
- The fact that the appellant has only a sixth or seventh grade education would severely limit the type of manual labor that he could perform.
- The BVA, although it mentioned the non-service-connected disabilities in its discussion, failed to set forth reasons why it was "not persuaded" that the appellant was unemployable based solely on his service-connected injuries.
- The record shows that the appellant has no employment history after leaving the service. Realistically, if he was discharged as being permanently disabled by an ankle injury, the reason for the discharge was that the army had no employment for him including "light manual labor."
- The BVA further erred by failing to address the different medical opinions expressed as to the appellant's unemployability.

- In assessing the appellant's unemployability, the BVA may be unable to determine whether the appellant's unemployability is caused by his non-service-connected disabilities or by his service-connected disabilities. If that is the case, then the evidence may be so evenly balanced that the doctrine of the benefit of the doubt found in 38 U.S.C. §5107(b) may apply.

TOWNSEND V. DERWINSKI, 1 VET. APP. 408 (1991)

In deciding *Townsend*, the court remanded the case to the BVA with instructions to specify the medical authority or medical evidence of record used to conclude that Mr. Townsend's foot condition was not aggravated while in the service. The remand order also directed the BVA to provide reasons or bases to explain why it denied the claim and instructed it to consider the Doctrine of Reasonable Doubt.

Mr. Townsend was discharged from the U.S. Army in 1970, having completed three years of active service including a combat tour in Vietnam. His entrance medical examination was silent as to any physical abnormalities of his feet. However, while in basic training he was treated for pain of the right foot. The examining physician noted in his record that the patient had "flat feet" and a navicular bar in his right foot. The record also contained a reference that the patient reported minimal trouble with his right foot before entering the Army. The doctor stated that Mr. Townsend was not qualified for service and should be separated. However, the patient stated he wanted to stay in the service. He was allowed to continue in basic training and upon graduation was given a permanent medical profile that would eliminate any activity that involved crawling, stepping, running, jumping, prolonged standing, or marching.

Despite a diagnosis of severe pes planus (flat feet) and a limited-duty profile, he was assigned to combat duty in Vietnam. His right foot condition was further aggravated by long periods of standing and heavy lifting duties. He was treated throughout his tour for foot pain. The separation medical examination noted "pes planus severe—see health record."

A claim was filed by the veteran for his right foot condition in 1983 and was subsequently denied by the local VARO. The letter of denial acknowledged that the entrance examination did not find anything wrong with his right foot and when discharged he was suffering from severe pes planus. They justified the denial of benefits based on an assumption: "By generally accepted medical principles, pes planus . . . [is] held to have preexisted service and [was] not aggravated thereby." Unfortunately, Mr. Townsend did not appeal this decision within one year of being notified of being denied benefits.

In 1989, the veteran tried to reopen his claim for a right flat foot condition. Again the VARO denied his action to obtain benefits. This time Mr. Townsend did file an appeal within the one-year time frame. His case was heard in early 1990 by the BVA and denied. The BVA held that "A review of the evidence of record reveals that, there having been no timely appeal, the originating agency's determination of March 1983 became final and in the absence of error, that determination is not subject to revision on the same factual basis." The BVA concluded that "1. A bilateral disorder was not incurred in or aggravated by service. 2. The originating agency's determination of March 1983 was final; the additional evidence received subsequent to that determination does not present a new factual basis so as to warrant the grant of service connection for a bilateral foot disorder."

The case was appealed to the Court of Veterans Appeals

and decided on July 25, 1991. The court reversed the BVA decision and remanded it. The court made these points when it sided with the veteran:

- A preexisting injury or disease will be considered to have been aggravated by active service where there is an increase in disability during such service, unless there is a specific finding that the increase in disability is due to the natural progress of the disease. 38 U.S.C. §1153 (1994).
- This provision is interpreted by 38 CFR §3.306(b) (1995): "(b) Wartime service; peacetime service after December 31, 1946. Clear and unmistakable evidence (obvious or manifest) is required to rebut the presumption of aggravation where the preservice disability underwent an increase in severity during service."
- When read together, these provisions state that once a claimant's disability increases in severity during service there is a presumption of aggravation (i.e., service connection), unless it can be established by clear and unmistakable evidence that the increase was due to the natural progression of the disease.
- The records show that the appellant's foot disorder increased in severity during service inclusive of the time of discharge.
- The BVA decision, without a discussion of the presumption of the way it is rebutted, found that there was no error in the VARO rating decision, which had also ignored the presumption and its rebuttal.
- The court has consistently ruled that the BVA must apply relevant law (even though 38 CFR §3.306(b) was not raised by the appellant).
- The BVA apparently relied solely on the "generally accept-

able medical principles" rationale given by the VARO when it denied the appellant's claim.

- The failure of the BVA to cite the medical authority or medical evidence in the record to support this conclusionary statement is not in accordance with the law.
- The BVA decision did not provide the necessary reasons or bases to explain its action.
- The BVA failed to consider the Doctrine of Reasonable Doubt in resolving the appellant's claim.

Chapter 11 Highlights

The Court of Appeals for Veterans Claims stated that the Doctrine of Reasonable Doubt is meant to be the easiest standard of proof found anywhere in the American system of jurisprudence. The court has told us that the adoption of this standard

is in keeping with the high esteem in which our nation holds those who have served in the Armed Services. It is in recognition of our debt to our veterans that society has through legislation taken upon its self the risk of error when, in determining whether a veteran is entitled to benefits, there is an approximate balance of positive and negative evidence. *By tradition and by statute, the benefit of doubt belongs to the veteran* [emphasis added].

It has been more than ten years since the court first addressed the issue of reasonable doubt in *Gilbert*. Have veterans benefited from this protection? The answer depends on what level of the bureaucracy is applying the standard. If a case is before the court, the standard of reasonable doubt definitely is scrutinized and applied. If the case is before the BVA, there is a very good chance that the standard will be applied. The BVA is directly under the oversight of the court, and if an appeal is filed with the court and the standard has not been properly applied, the appeal will be remanded to the BVA. However, this is where application of the standard of reasonable doubt practically ceases. Local VAROs have considerable difficulty correctly applying this concept to a claim action. They always say they considered the Doctrine of Reasonable Doubt but the evidence was not in favor of the veteran's claim. Yet the rating is totally silent as to how they arrived at this decision.

If a claim is denied, first request a copy of the complete rating decision and C&P Examination under the provisions of the Freedom of Information Act. Every report has at least two pages. Most ratings run four or five pages, depending on how many issues are being rated. They also include the rating schedule (code and percentage for each disability). Make certain the rating schedule and signature page are included as part of this report. If the local regional office fails to include these pages or any portion of the rating, contact your representative or senator and request his help in obtaining the missing page or pages. A VARO has no authority to withhold any portion of a requested document; it must provide the complete document.

Second, locate the statement concerning the application of reasonable doubt and determine exactly what evidence was used to deny the claim. A rating decision should be analyzed as follows:

• Did the VA obtain all my service medical records and VA medical records? If you did not provide this medical evidence with your claim, then you must request a complete copy of all the evidence used in considering your claim.

- Did the VA obtain additional evidence that I requested that would support the claim?
- Did the rating discuss all the favorable evidence filed with the claim?
- Did the VA rate all the disabilities I claimed? If not, did it explain why it failed to do so?
- Did the VA provide complete reasons or a basis for its findings? This includes identifying those findings it deems crucial to its decision and accounting for the evidence it finds persuasive or unpersuasive.
- If differences of medical opinions are expressed as to the issue of service connection, did the VA set forth the reasons why it was not persuaded by the evidence favorable to the claim?
- Did the VA cite its medical authority or medical evidence of record to support any conclusionary statement it may have made in the rating?

The third step is to reread the cases cited as part of this unit, especially *Fluharty* and *Townsend*. Remember, the VA cannot deny a benefit unless it can justify its decision. Now that local VAROs are permitted to use single-signature ratings as an everyday practice, the claimant must challenge every denied decision. Rating specialists have neither legal nor medical training to sufficiently qualify them to adjudicate complex medical and legal issues. Do not make the fatal error of assuming that their decision is just or in accord with the evidence or law.

The final step is to file a Notice of Disagreement. When the VA responds with a Statement of the Case, the appeal process is in the works. You have one year from the date of the VA's original notice of denial to submit your formal appeal. A formal appeal is your argument as to why benefits should have been granted.

Do not be cheated out of what is justly yours by law. Know the rules and do not give up in frustration. Seek a competent advocate to help you through the appeal process. One last thought: there are some advocates whose expertise ends at filling out forms. Search for an advocate who is knowledgeable of the VA's duty, can apply the concepts of case law to your case, knows where to find evidence to fight your case, and is able to understand the complexities of your medical problems.

APPENDIX A:
TABLE OF AUTHORITIES

Case Law

Statutes

Other Authorities

Regulations

APPENDIX B:
GLOSSARY OF ABBREVIATIONS

A

AFB	Air Force Base
AMA	American Medical Association
AMIE	Automated Medical Information Exchange System
AOJ	Agency of Original Jurisdiction where the claim was first adjudicated

B

BVA	Board of Veterans' Appeals

C

"C-number"	claim file number
CFR	Code of Federal Regulations
CHAMPUS	Civilian Health and Medical Program of the Uniformed Services
CHAMPVA	Civilian Health and Medical Program of the Veterans Administration
C&P	Compensation & Pension (Examination)
CSS #	indicates a claim number that uses social security number

D

DIC	Dependency and Indemnity Compensation
DRG	diagnostic related groups
DSWA	Defense Special Weapons Agency

F
FOIA   Freedom Of Information Act
FR   Federal Register

G
GPO   Government Printing Office

H
HMO   health maintenance organization

I
IB 11-56   *Physician's Guide For Disability Evaluation Examinations*

L
LOD   Line of Duty Investigation

M
MOD   medical officer of the day
MPR   Military Personnel Records

N
N/A   not applicable
NARA   National Archive and Records Administration
NPRC   National Personnel Records Center
NTPR   Nuclear Test Personnel Review

O
OGC   Office of the General Counsel
OHRE   Office of Human Radiation Experiments
OMPF   Official Military Personnel Files

P

POW	prisoner of war
PTSD	posttraumatic stress disorder

R

RIF	Reduction in Forces

S

SSA	Social Security Administration
SSOC	Supplemental Statement of the Case

T

TDY	Temporary Duty

U

USAF	U.S. Air Force
U.S.C.	United States Code
U.S.C.A.	United States Code Annotated

V

VA	Department of Veterans Affairs
VAMC	Department of Veterans Affairs Medical Center
VARO	Department of Veterans Affairs Regional Office
Vet. App.	Veterans Appeals (United States Court of Appeals for Veterans Claims)
VISN	Veterans Integrated Service Network

W

WWI	World War One
WWII	World War Two
WWW	World Wide Web

APPENDIX C:
GLOSSARY OF DEFINITIONS

A

Affidavit A written statement sworn before a notary public. When the claimant, family, or friends provide such testimony, the VA must accept the statement as evidence and give it proper weight.

Analagous rating A rating that is based on a similar condition.

Appeal A request for a review of an AOJ determination on a claim.

Appellant An individual who appeals an AOJ claim determination.

Armed forces U.S. Army, Navy, Marine Corps, Air Force, and Coast Guard.

B

Board of Veterans' Appeals BVA; the VA department that reviews benefit claim appeals and that issues decisions on those appeals.

Board member An attorney, appointed by the secretary of the Department of Veterans Affairs and approved by the president, who decides veterans benefits appeals.

C

Central office The director of the Compensation and Pension Service, VA central office, shall approve all VARO determinations establishing or denying POW status with the exception of those service departments' findings establishing that detention or internment was by an enemy government or its agents.

Chronicity Referring to a health problem, long duration or recurrence.

Claim A request for veterans benefits.

Claim number A number assigned by the VA that identifies a person who filed a claim; often called a "C-number."

Claim file The file containing all documents concerning a veteran's claim or appeal.

Compensable Entitled to compensation benefits.

Continuity of symptomatology A history of treatment of a health problem.

Court of Appeals for Veterans Claims An independent United States administrative court that reviews appeals of BVA decisions.

D

Date of receipt The date on which a claim, information, or evidence was received in the Department of Veterans Affairs, except as to the specific provisions of the Code of Federal Regulations for claims or evidence received in the State Department, the Social Security Administration, or Department of Defense as to initial claims filed at or prior to separation.

Decision The final product of the BVA's review of an appeal. Possible actions are to grant or deny the benefit or benefits claimed or to remand them to the AOJ for additional action.

Deposition A sworn statement before a notary.

Determination A decision on a claim made at the VARO.

DIC Compensation benefits granted to a surviving spouse resulting from a veteran's service-related death.

Discharge Separation, including retirement, from the active armed forces.

E
Evidence
>   **Fair preponderance of evidence** The evidence must be sufficient to prove that the evidence against the veteran's claim outweighs the evidence offered in support of the claim.
>   **Lay evidence** Evidence provided by a nonexpert.
>   **Preponderance of evidence** The VA must demonstrate that its evidence is superior to that which was introduced by the veteran before a claim may be denied.
>   **Probative evidence** Evidence that has a tendency to prove or actually prove an alleged entitlement.

F
File To submit in writing.

H
Hearing A meeting, similar to an interview, between an appellant and an official from the VA who will decide an appellant's case, during which testimony and other evidence supporting the case is presented. There are two types of personal hearings: regional office hearings (also called local office hearings) and BVA hearings.

Hostile force Any entity other than an enemy or foreign government or the agents of either whose actions are taken to further or enhance anti-American military, political, or economic objectives or views or to attempt to embarrass the United States.

I

In the line of duty Referring to an injury or disease incurred or aggravated during a period of active military, naval, or air service unless such injury or disease was the result of the veteran's own willful misconduct or, for claims filed after October 31, 1990, was a result of his abuse of alcohol or drugs. A service department finding that injury, disease, or death occurred in the line of duty will be binding on the VA unless it is patently inconsistent with the requirements of laws administered by the VA.

Issue A benefit sought on a claim or an appeal. For example, if an appeal seeks a decision on three different matters, the appeal is said to contain three issues.

L

Lay evidence See entry under Evidence.

Lay person A person that cannot give expert testimony related to the issue being adjudicated.

M

Marriage A marriage valid under the law of the place where the parties resided at the time of marriage, or the law of the place where the parties resided when the right to benefits accrued.

N

Non-service connected With respect to disability or death, that such disability was not incurred or aggravated, or that the death did not result from a disability incurred or aggravated, in line of duty in the active military, naval, or air service.

Notice A written notice sent to a claimant or payee at his latest address of record.

Notice of Disagreement A written statement expressing dissatisfaction or disagreement with a local VA office's determination on a benefit claim; must be filed within one year of the date of the regional office's decision.

P

Presumptive period The time frame in which an illness must manifest to a degree of 10 percent.

Prisoner of war A person who, while serving in the active military, naval, or air service, is forcibly detained or interned in the line of duty by an enemy or foreign government, the agents of either, or a hostile force.

Probative Referring to evidence that tends to prove a particular issue.

Proximate cause An event that caused an injury or disease and without such injury or exposure the disability would not have occurred.

R

Reasonable doubt In a VA claim action, the term implies certainty that must be applied before benefits can be denied. If the evidence pro and con is equal to or nearly equal to, the decision must be in favor of the claimant.

Rebut To contradict or oppose by formal legal argument.

Rebuttal of service incurrence Evidence which may be considered in rebuttal of a disease listed in 38 CFR §3.09. This evidence would refute the condition was service related.

Regional office A local VA office; there are 58 VA

regional offices throughout the United States and its territories.

Regional office hearing A personal hearing conducted by a VARO hearing officer. A regional office hearing may be conducted in addition to a BVA hearing.

Relevant Refers to evidence that is pertinent, relative, or connected to the point or target.

Remand To return an appeal to the regional office or medical facility where the claim originated.

Residuals A disability remaining from a disease or operation.

S

Separation The discharge or retirement of an individual from the service.

Service connection With respect to disability or death, that such disability was incurred or aggravated, or that the death resulted from a disability incurred or aggravated, in line of duty in the active military, naval, or air services.

State Each of the several states, territories, and possessions of the United States, the District of Columbia, and commonwealth of Puerto Rico.

Statement of the Case Prepared by the VARO, a summary of the evidence considered, as well as a listing of the laws and regulations used in deciding a benefit claim. It also provides information on the right to appeal a VARO's decision to the BVA.

Supplemental Statement of the Case A summary, similar to a Statement of the Case, that the VA prepares if a VA Form-9 contains a new issue or presents new evidence and the benefit is still denied. A Supplemental Statement of the Case will be provided when an appeal is returned (remanded) to the VARO by the BVA for new or additional action.

V

Vacate To reverse an original decision.

Veterans service organization An organization that represents the interest of veterans. Most veteran service organizations have specific membership criteria, although membership is not usually required to obtain assistance with benefit claims or appeals.

W

Wartime service The following dates are inclusive for formal periods of war in which a veteran will have been considered as serving during a wartime period: WWI— April 6, 1917–November 11, 1918 (veterans who served in Russia from April 6, 1917–July 7, 1921, are also considered wartime veterans); WWII—September 16, 1940–December 31, 1946; Korean Conflict—June 27, 1950–January 31, 1955; Vietnam Era—August 5, 1964–May 7, 1975 (those who served as advisors in Vietnam any time between February 28, 1961, and August 4, 1964, are also included); Persian Gulf War— August 2, 1990, to a date yet to be determined. Wartime service also means any time in which combat service was performed between January 1, 1947, and a date yet to be determined. Several examples would be the Berlin Air Lift, Lebanon Crisis, Grenada, Iranian Crisis, and Bosnia.

Willful misconduct An act involving conscious wrongdoing or known prohibited action (*malum in se* or *malum prohibitum*). A service department finding that injury, disease, or death was not due to misconduct will be binding on the Department of Veterans Affairs unless it is patently inconsistent with the facts and the requirement of laws administered by the Department of Veterans Affairs.

INDEX

ABOUT THE AUTHOR

Maj. John D. Roche, U.S. Air Force (Ret.), served in the Air Force as a bomber pilot, had combat duty in the Korean and Vietnam wars, and held a variety of administrative assignments. Subsequently, he worked for three years as a claims adjudication specialist for the Veterans Administration and as a veterans service officer for Pinellas County, Florida, where he was a tireless advocate for veterans and their families. Roche enjoyed one of the highest rates of wins on appeal in the state. This book, his first, is based on his experience as a successful practitioner, five years of independent research, and personal consultations with some 80,000 veterans and dependents. He lives in Palm Harbor, Florida.